GW00992419

THE
TILE ARTIST'S
MOTIF BIBLE

THE
TILE ARTIST'S
MOTIF BIBLE

200 DECORATIVE DESIGNS WITH STEP-BY-STEP
INSTRUCTIONS AND CHARTS

Jacqui Atkin

krause publications
An imprint of F+W Publications, Inc.
www.krausebooks.com

A QUARTO BOOK

First published in North America in 2007 by
Krause Publications
700 East State Street
Iola, WI 54990-0001

Copyright © 2007 Quarto Inc.

All rights reserved. No part of this publication may be
reproduced, stored in a retrieval system, or transmitted in
any form or by any means, electronic, mechanical,
photocopying, recording, or otherwise, without the
permission of the copyright holder in writing.

ISBN-10: 0-89689-438-X
ISBN-13: 978-0-89689-438-9

Library of Congress Catalog Card Number
2006934233

Conceived, designed, and produced by
Quarto Inc.
The Old Brewery
6 Blundell Street
London N7 9BH

QUAR:TAB

PROJECT EDITOR Donna Gregory
ART EDITOR AND DESIGNER Sheila Volpe
ASSISTANT ART DIRECTOR Penny Cobb
PICTURE RESEARCHER Claudia Tate
ILLUSTRATOR Kuo Kang Chen
PHOTOGRAPHER Ian Howes
INDEXER Sue Edwards

ART DIRECTOR Moira Clinch
PUBLISHER Paul Carslake

Manufactured by Pica Digital, Singapore
Printed by Midas Printing International Ltd, China

9 8 7 6 5 4 3 2 1

Contents

DESIGN & MOTIF DIRECTORY

Introduction

Tiles provide a practical and hard-wearing surface that will stand the test of time, and because they are both waterproof and heatproof, they make an especially practical surface covering for any number of interior and exterior spaces.

TILES THROUGH TIME

It is widely thought that tiles originated in the Near and Middle East about four thousand years ago, where they were used as architectural fixtures and decoration for interior walls, floors, and ceilings. Originally they would have been earth colored, but with the development of glaze, which probably came about as an extension of the glass-making process, tiles were able to take on colorful surfaces that allowed them to be laid in sophisticated and decorative patterns.

The first decorative tiles were made by the Egyptians, evidence of which can be seen in the stepped pyramid of the tomb of King Zoser

ABOVE Blue faience tiled panel from the pyramid of Djoser, Egypt (2650–2575 BCE) Sakkara.

RIGHT Detail of three figures hand-painted on tiles from Kerman, Iran.

LEFT Polychrome zellij tiles use geometric designs (from the Saadian Tombs Marrakesh).

BELOW Beautifully colored detail of an Islamic tile.

(2630–2611 BCE) at Sakkara, where the walls are lined with small, brightly colored blue tiles.

In later times, one of the major factors influencing the development and proliferation of decorative tiles through the millenniums was movement along the trade routes, especially the Silk Route from China, which directly influenced the Islamic ceramic style developed by Persian craftsmen in AD/50 In time this style included luster decoration, which produced a metallic sheen used to spectacular effect to decorate mosques, temples, and palaces.

European developments at this time were rudimentary by contrast, with the encaustic inlay technique being the only decorative style in use, and then only in religious buildings. It was not until the eighteenth century that the exotic tile decoration of the Middle East began to influence European production, and at roughly the same time, the East India Company were importing goods

LEFT Eighteenth-century Delft tile hand-painted in cobalt blue farm and yacht motif.

from Asia and the Orient, influencing Dutch tile-makers to develop the majolica technique known as "Delftware."

Until the middle of the eighteenth century all tiles were made by hand, at which time new printing techniques were developed, allowing the mass reproduction of very fine detail. Subsequently, production grew to meet the demands of the housing expansion brought about by the industrial revolution of the nineteenth century.

Tile production then went through several changes in the twentieth century, affected by the world wars and a return of the studio potter, making handmade tiles popular once again.

MAKING AND DECORATING TILES BY HAND

Today, you can buy tiles in a vast range of colors and patterns, but a truly original tile must be handmade. My purpose in this book is to provide you with the techniques necessary to interpret and reproduce the given images and motifs into your own ceramic format, to produce really individual tiles.

The book is arranged into easy-to-understand stages of the tile-making and decorating process, including clay choice and transferring the designs from the template to the surface of the tile. Guidelines are given for slip and glaze color, with some recipes, but much is open to personal interpretation, making the possibilities to create unique tiles even greater, so have fun experimenting.

BELOW Flowers, birds and insects are surrounded by blue and white Delft tiles.

How to use this book

200 tiles are featured in the Directory section (pages 58–251), organized into easy-to-access categories.

DESCRIPTION Information about the design.

INSTRUCTIONS Step-by-step instructions for making the tile.

MOTIF

92 Sgraffito Pear You could make tiles with the same background detail but without the motif, to intersperse with this tile and other fruit motifs for a really unique effect.

Fruits and vegetables

NUMBER Each tile is numbered.

Order of work

1 Prepare the tile and allow it to dry to leather hard.

2 Transfer the design to the surface of the tile and sgraffito the motif using a sgraffito tool, and the background detail using a loop tool.

PHOTOGRAPH Full color photograph of each tile.

3 After biscuit firing, apply white tin glaze to the tile then wipe it back until it only remains in the sgraffito areas. Fire to the recommended glaze temperature.

CLAY Red earthenware fired to 2,012°F (1,100°C) biscuit and 1,976°F (1,080°C) glaze

CLAY TYPE Clay type and firing temperature.

You will need
• Red earthenware clay
• Sgraffito tool
• Loop tool
• White tin glaze

YOU WILL NEED Materials and tools needed.

Arranging tiles
Randomly arrange these tiles will in a scheme of plain tiles with the same background detail.

DESIGN IDEA

CHART Gridded chart to enable you to transfer the design to your own tile.

TECHNIQUE

DIFFICULTY

1 **2**

see also kilns and firing **18–21** drying tiles **37** transferring motifs **53**

153

TECHNIQUE SYMBOLS Techniques used in the creation of the tile (see panel).

SEE ALSO cross refers reader to key techniques, explained in depth elsewhere in the book.

LAYOUT IDEAS Ideas for laying out the tiles in an interior scheme.

SKILL LEVEL On a scale of 1–3, 1 being easiest and 3 the most challenging.

ABOUT THE TECHNIQUE SYMBOLS

 slabbed 26–27

 commercially bought 54–55

 slip cast 30

 press molded/ low relief 28–29

 stencil 56–57

 sgraffito 35

 paper resist 33

 paint-on glaze 44

 slip trailing 34

 single glaze 40–42

 mono printing 50

 tube lining 36

 tile paints 55

 on-glaze enamels 48

 multiple glazes 40–42

 inlay 35

 impressing 37

 luster 49

 intaglio printing 52

 majolica 44

 sealing 55

Glaze recipes
These glaze recipes represent those used on many tiles in this book. If you prefer not to mix your glazes from the raw ingredients, your pottery supplier will be able to advise you on suitable pre-prepared alternatives.

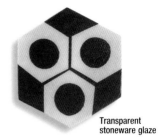

Transparent stoneware glaze

Transparent earthenware lead glaze

Lead bi-silicate	65
Whiting	10
Potash feldspar	15
China clay	10

Fire to 1,976°F (1,080°C).
This is a versatile, transparent glaze that can be colored by oxides or stains for variation. Add 3 percent red iron oxide and 0.5 percent manganese dioxide to make orange; 5 percent cobalt oxide to give a good blue, and 3 percent copper oxide to give deep green.

Earthenware tin glaze

Lead bi-silicate	26
Borax frit	7
Ball clay	6
China clay	4
Tin oxide	3
Bentonite	1

Fire to 1,980–2,050°F (1,080– 1,120°C)
This is a stable white tin glaze ideal for red clay and majolica decoration. It breaks nicely over texture to reveal a rich red color.

Transparent stoneware

| Cornish stone | 85 |
| Whiting | 15 |

Plus 2 percent Bentonite

Fire to 2,300–2,336°F (1,260–1,280°C) with a 30-minute soak.
Add 4 percent tin oxide to make white; 4 percent glaze stain generally makes a good color but you will need to experiment for best results.

Dolomite stoneware

Potash feldspar	30
Dolomite	20
Whiting	15
China clay	20
Flint	5

Fire to 2,309°F (1,265°C).
This glaze is good over an oxide wash and in combination with other glazes.

RAKU GLAZES

Turquoise luster glaze

High alkaline frit	50
Borax frit	20
Copper oxide	4
Bentonite	3

Fire to 1832°F (1000°C).
This glaze produces a good turquoise when applied thickly and copper-red luster when heavily reduced in sawdust.

Raku transparent glaze

High alkali frit	46
Borax frit	46
China clay	8

Looks good over white clay bodies—good crackle.

Raku transparent glaze

Earthenware tin glaze

Transparent earthenware glaze

HEALTH AND SAFETY

When working with clay and other related materials:

1 Never eat, drink, or smoke in the workshop.

2 Always work in a suitably ventilated room with easy-to-clean, impermeable work surfaces, and facilities for washing close by.

3 Avoid generating airborne dust. It is better to prevent dust than to try to control it. To minimize hazards:
• Clean up spills immediately. This applies to liquids as well as powders because all materials become dust when they have dried. Spills on the floor also pose the risk of slipping.
• Clean all tools and equipment at the end of the working day.
• Use a vacuum cleaner with a filter for fine dust, not a brush, to clean all surfaces. After vacuuming, wash all surfaces.

4 Wear gloves when handling any coloring agents or oxides.

5 Wear a respirator (face mask) when handling powders.

6 Wear protective clothing. Try not to wipe dirty hands on your apron, as this will create dust when dry. Wash work clothing regularly.

7 Store dry materials in airtight, plastic containers to prevent bags breaking open and spilling dust into the atmosphere.

8 When sanding or fettling (trimming or cleaning) dry or biscuit-fired pots, wear a respirator and goggles to protect your nose and eyes.

9 Check that your tetanus immunization is up to date. Remember that clay is essentially dug from the ground and may carry bacteria that can cause infection in open wounds.

10 Keep a first-aid kit in the workshop. Protect cuts and scratches from contact with any ceramic materials.

Always wear a mask when doing "dusty" jobs, such as glaze mixing or fettling Change filters regularly.

DANGEROUS MATERIALS

Some materials used in pottery as colorants for clays and glazes can be harmful if breathed in or ingested. Some studies suggest that certain materials can even be absorbed through the skin. Be sure to wear the appropriate protection when handling the following materials. Pottery suppliers should always provide the relevant health and safety data for their products, and information relating to each material should be printed on the container. Be sure to read it!

Highly toxic

Lead, cadmium, antimony, and barium.

Use with care

• All colorants, especially copper oxide and carbonate, cobalt oxide and carbonate, chromium oxide, lithium oxide, zinc, strontium, nickel oxide, and slip and glaze stains.

• Borax, boron, boric acid, silica, quartz, flint, feldspar, China clay, ball clay, whiting, and dolomite.

Tools and equipment
You really only need very basic tools and equipment to make tiles successfully. The examples shown are the minimum you will require to get started but you can choose more from the suggested list as you gain experience.

1

2

3

4

5

6

Basic tools (pictured)
1 Rolling pin
2 Roller guides
3 Craft or potters' knife
4 Sgraffito tool
5 Cutting wire
6 Kidneys, metal and rubber
7 Slip trailer
8 Brushes
9 Sponges
10 A card template of the tile or card to make templates from

Other suggested tools
Hardwood modeling tool
Forged steel tool (used for carving plaster detail)
Small double-ended strip-turning tool
Cup sieve
Large lawn sieve
Flat-edged brush
Large Chinese brush, excellent for decorative brushwork
Long-handled, wide "soft hake" brush for applying decoration or glaze

7

8

9

10

**Decorating ready—
glazed commercial tiles**
Spray-on glue and
lacquer
White acrylic paint
Cutting mat
Tracing paper
Transfer paper
Craft knife
Pencil
Mineral spirits
Colored acrylic paints
Removable adhesive
Cotton swabs
Paintbrushes
Synthetic and natural
sponges
Enamel paints
Glazed tiles
Masking tape

Stencil
brushes
Stencils
Stencil card
Ballpoint pen

Clay bodies
In its natural state, clay can be found almost anywhere in the world. Clay in its raw state is not very pliable, making it difficult to work with and requiring the addition of other materials to make it supple.

The basic components of clay are silica and alumina. Natural clay is formed over millions of years from feldspathic or granite rocks, which have been decomposed through the action of weather and glaciers. Clays that are still where they were originally formed are known as residual or primary clays, and are fairly rare. The most important primary clay is kaolin (China clay). It is very pure and white with a large particle size that makes it very short (nonplastic), and thus unsuitable for use on its own. Bentonite is an extremely fine, plastic primary clay, which is added to shorter clays to increase their plasticity.

Clays that have been further eroded and weathered are known as secondary or sedimentary clays. They have been moved from their original source by water, wind, or glacier. Such clays have fine particles and are very plastic. Ball clays are included in this group. In the process of traveling, the clays pick up minerals and impurities, making them suitable only for low-firing temperatures.

CLAY TYPES
Before choosing a clay for your project, you should consider how it will be fired, and the final result you hope to achieve. Ask your supplier to recommend a suitable clay.

Here is a selection of commercial clays in their raw state and in their three main groups. The color can change dramatically after firing, but your supplier should be able to show you fired samples before you buy.

Earthenware
The most common and the least expensive clay, earthenware has a high iron content, giving it a rich, rusty color. Earthenware has a firing temperature of 1,832–2,156°F (1,000–1,180°C). It does not vitrify (become glasslike), and so needs to be glazed. The glaze must be craze-resistant, to prevent liquids from being absorbed into the clay body.

White earthenware makes an ideal choice for decoration with colored slips or stains. It has a firing range of 1,940–2,156°F (1,060–1,180°C).

Red earthenware
Fires to a rich terra-cotta—particularly suited to various forms of slip decoration.

White earthenware
Gray before firing and creamy white after—used in the same way as the red variety, but gives a brighter color response for decoration.

Black earthenware
Black before firing—and chocolate brown to black after—provides an exciting alternative to red and white varieties.

Stoneware

Stoneware clays are much stronger than earthenware; their density and hardness when fired give them their name. They can be fired to very high temperatures of 2,192–2,372°F (1,200–1,300°C), which cause the clay particles to fuse (vitrify), making the surface impervious to fluids. Items only need to be glazed for hygienic, decorative, or aesthetic purposes.

There is a wide selection of stoneware clays available, in colors ranging from white to dark brown and compositions ranging from very smooth to very coarse. Most bodies are prepared from a mixture of plastic clays and minerals.

White stoneware
Fires to white—medium textured, containing several grades of molochite (calcined China clay).

Special stoneware
Blend of low shrinkage clays and calcined China clay—medium texture, excellent plasticity, low shrinkage, and a wide firing range fires to an ivory or off-white color.

Grogged stoneware
Heavily grogged—textured but highly plastic—firing to a speckled gray-buff color—suited to slab work—good choice for Raku.

Porcelain
The ultimate white-firing stoneware clay—generally very fine textured.

Porcelain

Porcelain is the whitest firing of all the clay bodies and the purest. It can be fired up to 2,372°F (1,300°C); at this temperature it is very hard and nonporous and can be incredibly translucent if worked thinly.

Porcelain is the most difficult clay to handle and is not the best material for the beginner. In addition, porcelain can distort significantly in the firing. Practice and a delicate touch will enable you to master this clay, though you can use white stoneware or earthenware instead.

Clay storage

Keep clay stored in tightly sealed plastic bags to retain moisture, in a dark, cool, frost-free place. Even in these conditions, the clay will eventually dry out, so check it from time to time. If it gets too hard, wrap it in an old, wet towel and seal in a plastic bag for a few days. If too hard to handle, allow to dry out totally and then reclaim it.

Clay consistency

The consistency of clay directly relates to the type of tile being made and the technique to be used. Clays should be soft enough to mold in the fingers without being sticky. Soft clay can be firmed up by kneading on a porous surface to remove excess water. Hard clay can often be saved by wedging in softer clay.

Ready-made clays

Clay shrinks as it dries and again when fired. You can expect your clay to shrink between 10 and 15 percent, depending on its type and the firing temperature. Clay can warp as it dries, but this can be alleviated by the addition of sand or grog.

Pottery suppliers provide information about shrinkage rates. Ask your supplier for samples to test for suitability.

RECLAIMING CLAY

One of the best things about working with clay is that there is very little waste. Until it is fired, it can be reprocessed again and again without detriment. Reclaim each type of clay in separate buckets, or save them together to make a mixed body. Always test the mixed clay body before making tiles.

Shrinkage

To measure your clay for shrinkage, roll out some sample slabs and cut them into 6-in. (15-cm) strips. Draw a 4-in. (10-cm) line down the center of the strips. Measure the line when the clay has dried, after it has been biscuit fired, and after it has been fired to its top temperature. When testing several clays, number the samples because fired clays can look very similar. Make a note of your results for future reference.

Reclaiming clay

1 Allow the clay to dry out completely. Break it into small pieces and place it in a large plastic container.

2 Completely cover the clay with warm water and allow it to break down overnight—this process is called slaking down.

3 Siphon off the excess water with a slip trailer. Give the clay slurry a little mix and transfer it to a plaster bat to form a layer about 2 in. (5 cm) thick.

4 Check the clay from time to time. When it has dried to a stage where it can be lifted easily from the bat, turn the clay over so that the wetter slurry on the surface comes into contact with the plaster. When the clay has firmed up to a workable consistency, remove it from the bat and wedge it (see above).

Wedging

Wedging mixes the clay and removes air bubbles that could cause the clay to shatter when fired. This technique can be used to blend two or more clay types together or to combine hard and soft layers of a particular clay.

1 Slice the two blocks of clay into sheets with a cutting wire. Stack in alternate layers. Beat the pile into a brick with your hand.

CLAY PREPARATION

As with many other crafts, preparation is vital for a successful outcome.

KNEADING

Kneading is essential to even out the clay body and remove air bubbles, which can cause bloating or explosions during firing. Badly prepared clay will lead to very disappointing results.

Water constantly evaporates from clay. Kneading redistributes the water. Prepare only enough clay to complete the project and keep it sealed in plastic until needed.

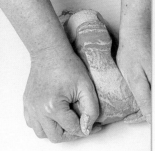

2 Position the cutting wire under the raised end, as close to the center as possible. Cut the block in half.

3 Lift one half then throw it forcibly on top of the other half. Beat the clay back to a brick shape. Repeat until the two clays are completely combined.

Ox-head kneading

Many potters find this the easier of the two methods.

Position the hands on opposite sides of the clay mass with the heels over the top and the fingers wrapped around the sides. Push the clay down and away from the body, digging the palms into the clay so that a raised mass remains in the center. Roll the clay back toward the body and reposition the hands slightly forward. Repeat until smooth and well mixed with no air pockets.

Spiral kneading

This technique is more difficult to master than ox-head kneading, but it is useful for larger amounts of clay.

Place your hands on opposite sides of a roughly rounded mass of clay. With your right hand, push down on the clay while rolling it forward. Contain the clay with your left hand to prevent sideways movement. Use your left hand to rotate the clay mass after each forward movement. Try to develop a rhythm as you work.

Kilns and firing

Without doubt, the kiln is the most expensive item you are ever likely to need for making tiles. Do not rush into a decision but look at all the available models offered by as many suppliers as possible. There can be quite substantial differences in price between suppliers for similar models.

Beginners are generally best advised to fire in an electric kiln because the outcome of the firing is the most predictable. All the projects in this book were fired in an electric kiln; some had their second firing in a Raku kiln.

Electric kilns are generally the most suitable for urban environments because they fire cleanly, whereas gas or wood kilns create fumes and smoke. Electric kilns are available in a vast range of sizes, the smallest of which can be fired in a domestic situation. Sophisticated firing controllers will program every stage of the firing and mean that you do not have to be with the kiln while it fires.

Top-loading electric kilns
Top-loading kilns are ideal for the beginner because they tend to be cheaper to buy, will fit into small-scale workshops, and are easier to install.

Front-loading kilns
Generally, front-loading kilns have a more solid metal framework and the firebrick wall is more substantial, which means it retains heat for much longer. This type of kiln is much harder wearing than the top-loading version but is more expensive to buy and install. It is also much heavier.

POINTS TO CONSIDER

• Accessibility to your premises. The kiln must fit through the door.
• The scale of your work and the quantity you produce. If you need to fire something in a hurry and your kiln is big, you will waste energy.
• Safety aspects. A kiln should not be in the room where you work. If it has to be, you should not be in the room while it is firing. Firing overnight can be the solution. A kiln should be located so you have enough space to move around it and away from flammable materials or structures.
• Power supply to your workshop. Some small kilns can be plugged into your normal household supply, but the bigger the kiln, the greater the power supply required.
• The strength of the floor in your workshop.

FIRING YOUR KILN

All objects made in clay have to be fired to make them permanent and functional. During firing, the real alchemy of pottery happens as the raw clay goes through a chemical change and becomes ceramic.

Beginners often find the prospect of firing their work daunting, but it is not a mystery and your confidence will build with experience. It will help if you record the results of your firing. Note all the details of your work, like glaze combinations, thickness of application, or decorative techniques.

You can easily forget what you did on a tile to make it fabulous—if you did not make a note, it can never be repeated.

Pottery generally has two firings: the first bisque or biscuit firing hardens the clay in preparation for secondary treatments like glaze; the second glaze firing is usually at a higher temperature and adds a protective and decorative coat. The glaze firing may be to earthenware or stoneware temperatures.

KILN FIRING TIMES AND TEMPERATURES

This kiln chart shows the approximate cycles recommended for successful firing of your tiles.

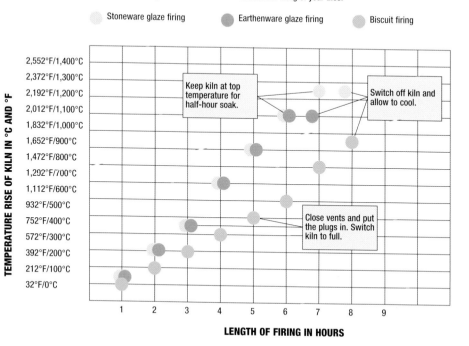

● Stoneware glaze firing   ● Earthenware glaze firing   ● Biscuit firing

TEMPERATURE RISE OF KILN IN °C AND °F

2,552°F/1,400°C
2,372°F/1,300°C
2,192°F/1,200°C
2,012°F/1,100°C
1,832°F/1,000°C
1,652°F/900°C
1,472°F/800°C
1,292°F/700°C
1,112°F/600°C
932°F/500°C
752°F/400°C
572°F/300°C
392°F/200°C
212°F/100°C
32°F/0°C

Keep kiln at top temperature for half-hour soak.

Switch off kiln and allow to cool.

Close vents and put the plugs in. Switch kiln to full.

1   2   3   4   5   6   7   8   9

LENGTH OF FIRING IN HOURS

KILN SUPPORTS AND PACKING

Kilns are packed using shelves and supports. Tubular supports are available in different sizes and heights and are stackable. Alternatively, you could use a tile crank, which is a specially designed refractory frame that will support a multiple number of tiles.

caption to above and right

caption to left and below

Placing ware in a kiln

When packing a biscuit kiln, objects can be placed in contact with each other and directly on the shelves. Tiles fired lying flat should be bedded on fine white sand (silica sand) to reduce the friction between the shelf and the clay body as they shrink. However, where possible, tiles should be biscuit fired standing on their edges. If they lie flat, the surface in contact with the shelf tends to bake harder and will contract slightly more than the upper surface, causing the tiles to bow upward.

In a glaze firing the glazed surfaces must be kept apart and not allowed to come into contact with any of the kiln furniture. A molten glaze will stick to any surface it touches, and if applied thickly, it can flow down over an unglazed edge. Kiln furniture can be protected from glaze contamination by applying a thin layer of high alumina wash (bat wash) to the surface.

An efficient way to stack tiles in a kiln is to use cranks. These are frames made of refractory material with three uprights held in position with a base and top plate. The uprights have evenly spaced pegs or lugs that in a low-temperature firing can support the tiles directly. With higher-temperature firings where the tiles might possibly warp, they must be loaded into the crank on small kiln bats.

PACKING A KILN FOR GLAZE FIRING

It is essential that the tiles do not touch one another. The kiln shelf must be coated with kiln wash to prevent glaze drips sealing the tiles onto the shelf. This is especially important for high-temperature firings. Kiln wash can be bought from your supplier or made from a mix of two parts alumina and one part China clay.

RAKU FIRING

The term "Raku" comes from the Japanese for happiness or enjoyment. It is an incredibly exciting and spectacular method of firing.

Raku kilns

Raku kilns can be built from firebricks or high-temperature insulating bricks. For more rapid firings, the kiln can be made from metal drums or wire-mesh cages and lined with ceramic fiber for insulation. Commercial gas burners are widely available and make firing quick, clean, and easy. Ask your supplier for details.

Firing procedure

Normally, open, grogged clays with good thermal-shock properties are used for Raku. The tiles are given a normal biscuit firing to 1,832°F (1,000°C) before being glazed and placed in the Raku kiln, which is most often fired using propane gas. The firing usually takes place outside because of the fumes. The tiles are rapidly fired until the glaze melts. Raku glazes melt at 1,472–1,832°F (800–1000°C), and firing usually takes 20–30 minutes. The tiles are lifted, still red-hot and glowing, from the kiln with tongs, and placed in drums of wood shavings. Because of the rapid cooling process, the tiles undergo intense thermal shock, which causes the glaze to craze, allowing smoke to penetrate through to the clay body. This gives the familiar crackle effect.

Tips for success

• Have absolutely everything you need ready before starting the firing.
• Make sure that the reduction bin is easy to access when you lift the work from the kiln.
• Position the kiln on a good flat surface.
• Have someone with you when you fire; it is safer and much more fun to share the experience.

SAFETY

Raku firing involves working with tiles at extreme temperatures and can be hazardous. To reduce the risk, you should have adequate gloves, protective clothing, masks, goggles, and tongs to lift the tiles from the kiln. Keep a bucket of water or a fire extinguisher close by in case of accidents.

Mold making
Making a tile from a mold is the best way to reproduce an image that needs to be made in larger numbers.

MIXING PLASTER FOR MOLD MAKING

Plaster molds can be incredibly useful to the potter who wants to be able to reproduce, quickly and accurately, a tile that cannot be easily made using hand-building methods. Making molds can seem daunting to the beginner, but once you have learned how to mix the plaster you are halfway to mastering the technique.

Accurately weighing and measuring the plaster and water will ensure that you get the mix right the first time, but judging the amount required for a particular project takes practice. See below for weights and measures. Potter's plaster is widely available from ceramic suppliers.

Plaster/water ratio

1 ½ lbs (675 g) plaster
1 pint (575 ml) water
This will give a strong mix for most pottery uses.

SAFETY NOTE

• NEVER wash excess plaster down the sink as it will set in the pipe and cause a blockage.
• Wipe excess plaster from your hands with newspaper before washing them, again to avoid blockages.
• Use newspaper to clean out your plaster bucket immediately after use.
• Wear rubber or latex gloves to mix the plaster if your skin is sensitive.
• It is advisable to wear a face mask when mixing plaster if you are concerned about inhaling the dust.

Mixing plaster

1 Pour the measured water into a bucket or large bowl. Weigh out the required amount of plaster into another dry container.

Carefully sprinkle the plaster powder into the water, adding it gradually and evenly until the powder breaks the surface of the water.

Shake the bucket gently to make sure the plaster seeps down into the water. Allow the mixture to stand for a minute or two to allow the plaster to absorb the water fully.

2 Stir the mixture gently with your hand to remove any lumps. Every so often, wiggle your hand at the bottom of the mixture to release any trapped air bubbles.

If bubbles rise to the surface, scoop them off carefully with your hand and transfer them onto newspaper or, preferably, into a pre-lined bin, which will make disposal much easier later.

Keep testing the viscosity of the mixture. When it no longer runs off your fingers, or is obviously thickening, it is ready.

MAKING A MULTI-FUNCTIONAL MOLD FOR SLIP CASTING OR PRESS MOLDING

Making a mold for a tile is not only an excellent way of mass producing a specific design exactly, but it also gives you the choice of either slip casting, which will give very sharp definition to the detail of the tile, or press molding for a more subtle finish.

If you want to make a plain mold without a relief surface, simply cut out a clay tile and cast it in plaster in the same way as demonstrated below. Plain molds are perfect for slip casting, as a lot of tiles can be made quickly.

Transferring the design

1 Roll out a slab of clay and cut to a 3-in. (15-cm) square. Transfer the tile to a nonabsorbent board which is at least 2 in. (5 cm) larger then position your paper design over the clay. Using a pencil, transfer the pattern to the surface by tracing over the lines.

2 Use thin coils of clay to build up some areas of the pattern to form the relief taking care not to create undercuts, which would trap the plaster and make it impossible to release the tile from the mold. Use slab offcuts to build up other areas and sgraffito line detail to delineate where appropriate. Add fine texture detail with a pointed wooden tool.

3 Build a thick slab wall or cottle around the model, allowing a 25 mm gap all the way around, and secure the wall with coils of soft clay. Mix 675 g of plaster to 570 ml of water (see page 22), then pour the plaster mixture over the model.

4 Agitate a flattened hand gently over the plaster in the cottle to raise any air bubbles and allow the mold to harden. Once the plaster has heated up and cooled down again, remove the cottle. Bevel the edges of the mold with a rasp blade and carefully remove the clay model.

DRYING THE MOLD

Allow the mold to dry out somewhere warm, propped up to allow air to circulate freely. It should only take a day or two to dry.

MAKING SPRIG MOLDS

Sprig molds are technically a form of decoration, since they are added to a finished form to provide low-relief detail. Probably the most famous example is Wedgwood's jasperware, which has white sprig work on a colored background (usually blue or green). Sprigs can be cast from a clay model or from found objects, and this project demonstrates how to make both kinds. Sprigs are quick and easy to produce, and it is a good idea to make several at a time so that you have a selection to choose from.

Generally speaking, the clay you use for sprigs should be the same as the body clay, or a stained version, to avoid possible shrinkage problems. It is usual to discard the first cast from a new mold because it can pick up any specks of plaster left behind on the surface and cause the work to explode when fired. This also applies to slip casting.

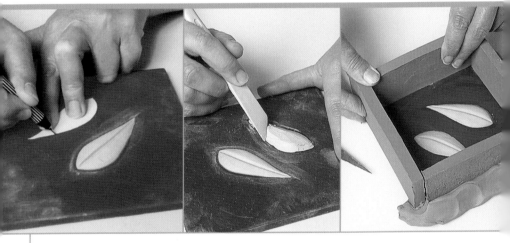

Making a sprig model from clay

1 To make a sprig from a clay model first transfer the outline of the motif to the surface of an old tile or other nonabsorbent surface.

2 Build up the shape of the motif with soft clay taking care not to create undercuts.

3 Secure a thick clay cottle around the model then cast the sprig in plaster following the method shown on page 23.

Tips for success

• Holes in a mold caused by bubbles in the plaster can be filled by being sprayed with water and then carefully filled to the brim with a sprinkling of plaster. When the plaster begins to set, the area can be scraped over with a kidney or modeling tool to smooth it off to the same level as the rest of the mold.

• Soft soap—a special liquid soap used in mold-making—is obtainable from pottery suppliers and needs to be diluted. Use 50 percent boiling water to 50 percent soap, and store the mixture in a screw-top jar.

• If you find it is too difficult to model fine detail onto a tiny sprig, scale the sprig up to a manageable size and then dry and fire it, either to biscuit or to the clay's top temperature, depending on the reduction in size required. The model can then be cast in plaster with all the detail in place.

Making sprigs from found objects

1 You can also use a found object for casting—a sea shell, button, old piece of jewelry, or any item that can be cast without presenting a problem of undercuts will do. Here, an ammonite is used. Embed the object in clay on another tile or board, and build up the level around the shape so that the sprig, when cast, will not be too thick. Model the clay around the object with a rubber kidney to form a level shelf about ½ inch (13 mm) wide, taking care to avoid undercuts.

2 Apply several coats of mold makers' size or soft soap to the surface of the model. This is done by brushing the soap over the model then wiping it back with a damp cloth. It prevents the plaster from sticking to the model. Build a wall around the model and cast in plaster as before. It is easier and more economical to make several sprigs at once to prevent plaster wastage. Finish off the sprig molds in the same way as the tile molds and allow to dry before use.

Slabbing
Slabbing is the quickest and easiest method by which to make tiles and requires only the most basic tools to get started.

Tips for successful slabbing

• To avoid air bubbles, always make sure that your clay has been very thoroughly wedged prior to rolling out.

• Form the lump of clay into a rough square shape to make rolling easier.

• If, in the process of rolling, you notice small air bubbles trapped in the clay, pierce them with a potter's pin. Roll over the surface again, making sure the guides are still in place to avoid altering the thickness of the slab.

Keep an even pressure on the rolling pin.

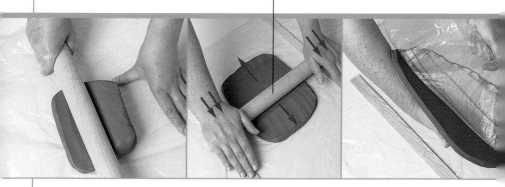

Rolling slabs

1 Lay the clay on a sheet of clean plastic. Using evenly weighted strokes, beat the clay with a rolling pin. Work systematically from one side of the block to the other. This helps reduce the initial bulk of the block of clay and drive out any air that may still be trapped in the clay.

Lift the block of clay off the plastic sheet. Turn it over and through 90 degrees. Repeat.

2 Reposition the clay on the plastic sheet with a roller guide positioned on each side so that the ends of the rolling pin can rest on them to gauge the final thickness of the slab.

Position the pin in the middle of the block and then roll away from your body and back again. It will not be possible to roll the slab in one try. Roll until you feel a natural resistance to any further rolling. This is a good indication that the slab needs to be turned.

3 To turn the slab, lift it in place on the sheet of plastic. Turn it over to rest on the opposite hand. Very carefully peel the plastic off the back of the slab and replace it in position on the work surface.

It is very important to remove the plastic sheet in this way to avoid ripping or distorting the slab.

MAKING TILES FROM SLABS

There are several ways of making tiles. They can be cut from rolled out slabs of clay, using a template or a tile-cutter, or pressed into a mold.

It is important to dry your tiles slowly and evenly before firing to prevent the clay from warping. Some potters dry their tiles on wire racks so that air can circulate around them at all times, while others dry them between weighted boards. Using a grogged clay body will help reduce the tendency to warp.

Lower the wire as you cut each slab.

Using templates

The simplest method of making tiles is to roll a slab of clay as shown on page 26, and then cut around paper or cardboard templates. Your tiles do not have to be square. However, if you make more complicated designs, it is important to measure and cut out templates accurately for a good fit.

Using a harp

A clay harp allows you to cut evenly thick slabs of clay. When cutting a block of clay, you lower the wire to the next notch as each slab is cut. Although a harp is not essential, it is very useful if you intend to make a lot of tiles. The tiles will still need to be cut to shape.

Using a tile cutter

You will still have to roll or harp the slabs of clay, but the tiles will be identical in size when you use a tile cutter. It is a useful tool if you want to make a lot of tiles quickly.

Press molding
Press molding is another quick method of making, generally requiring only roughly made slabs of clay because of the nature of the process.

USING A HARP TO CUT SLABS

A harp is a useful tool for cutting a number of slabs quickly for press molding but you should only buy a harp if you intend to use it extensively as rolling is an equally valid if somewhat slower method of making tiles.

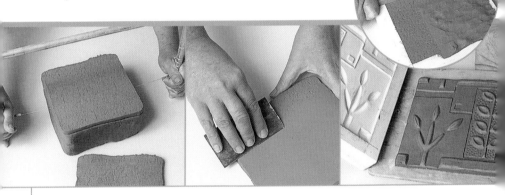

Cutting slabs using a harp

1 Wedge a large block of clay and form into a 6-in. (15-cm) cube. Place on a smooth work surface. Set the wire on the harp at an upper level that corresponds with a point just below the top of the block. Stand the harp on the opposite side of the block, holding firmly at the base of each side, and draw back through the clay toward you. Lift the slab off the block and put to one side. Move the wire down to the next level at each side of the harp and cut another slab. Repeat.

2 Smooth over the surface of the slab with a metal or rubber kidney before turning it over and pressing it firmly into the mold making sure it fits into the corners well as well as into the detail of the pattern in the plaster mold.

3 To trim off the excess clay, working in several stages, place a roller guide over the surface of the mold and draw it across using your thumbs to grip the sides. Work from the center outward. When all the clay is removed, turn the tile out in the same way as the slip-cast version (see page 30) and dry in the same way.

USING SPRIGS TO CREATE A LOW RELIEF

Tiles are wonderful surfaces to decorate. However, they do not have to be flat. Sprigs will create quick and interesting low relief detail.

To neaten around the edge of each sprig, remove excess slip with a wooden modeling tool or a damp paintbrush.

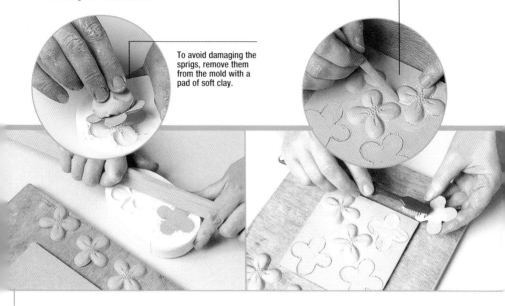

To avoid damaging the sprigs, remove them from the mold with a pad of soft clay.

Making sprigs

1 Press a small amount of soft clay into the sprig mold, making sure it fills the space thoroughly. Remove the excess clay by dragging a roller guide over the surface. Make sure the guide is flat on the plaster mold and take care not to pull the clay out of the mold. You may need to practice a little.

2 Arrange the sprigs on the tile. Score around each one with a pointed tool to mark its position.

Score and slip the marked positions and the underside of each sprig. Fix the sprigs securely in place while squeezing out any air.

Slip casting Using a low relief mold this gives the sharpest definition of pattern and a good way of reproducing multiples of one tile.

MAKING TILES FROM CASTING SLIP

Casting slip is a clay body in liquid form, enabling it to be poured into molds so that repeat shapes can be made. The slip should not shrink too much when it dries and should have a good dry strength for handling.

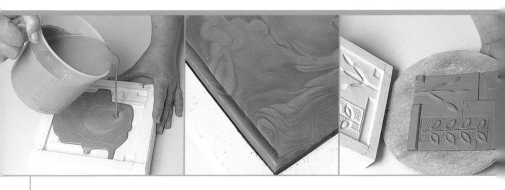

Making tiles from casting slip

1 When the mold is dry, you can start to produce a batch of tiles. First, mix the casting slip to a liquid consistency. Transfer the slip to a pitcher to make it easier to pour into the mold. Fill the mold with slip and replenish it from time to time to keep the surface level. Let the slip firm up in the mold until the clay shows no marks when it is touched. This can take any time from 30 minutes on, depending on a variety of factors.

2 The easiest way to judge that the tile is ready for removal is when the clay begins to shrink away from the edges of the mold. The clay used here is white earthenware (although it looks buff-colored in its liquid state). It can be cast and removed from the mold in about one hour, depending on the surrounding temperature. This allows several tiles to be cast in a day, although the mold quickly becomes saturated when in constant use and must be dried out thoroughly after each session of casting.

3 To remove the tile from the mold, place a bat over the surface and turn both over before lifting the mold off. This avoids distorting the shape. The mold is now ready to use again.

Dry the tiles slowly, preferably on a wire rack to allow free circulation of air that will prevent the shape from distorting. Alternatively they can be dried between boards but move them around from time to time so that, again, they dry evenly.

Decorating handmade tiles

There are many methods for decorating handmade tiles but we begin with slip decorating, which allows a great deal of scope for personal interpretation.

SLIP

Slip is the most common decorative technique applied to raw clay. Slip is simply liquid clay. The consistency of the slip will vary, depending on the job it has to do and the requirements of your particular decoration.

For many potters, a pure white slip provides the basis for decoration, giving a white background onto which colors can be painted for a brighter finish. A white slip can also have commercially made stains added; these make a range of colored clays for slip painting before using a transparent glaze to liven the surface and add a shiny finish. These colors are deceptive in their raw state, because they do not develop their true color until fired. Always test-fire slips before using them on your tiles.

Preparing slip

1 Slips must be able to adhere to the clay body, and, more importantly, shrink at a similar rate. A good, white-burning ball clay is usually a good bet and can be used on its own.

Measure out the powdered clay into a bucket and gradually add the water mixing as you pour it in. An average mix would be 4 ½ pints (2 liters) of water to 2.2 lb (1 kg) of dry, powdered clay.

2 Mix the clay thoroughly until it becomes creamy. Rub the mix through your fingers to squash any lumps out, and strain the slip through an 80-s mesh strainer to ensure an even, smooth consistency. For most painted applications, slip should be like a thick cream, and like a thin cream for dipping or pouring.

Mixing colors for slip

To add color to the slips, weigh out the required percentage of stain, add it to the dry, powdered clay and mix in well before adding the water. Color the slips using metal oxides added in small proportions, usually between 2 and 5 percent. A higher percentage of stains must be added to achieve similar intensity—additions of about 10 percent are common.

STORING AND APPLYING SLIP

The following three techniques represent the most common methods of applying slip. Whichever method you choose (apart from dipping), you will need to apply several coats to achieve an even covering, otherwise the clay body will show through. It will help if you store your slips in transparent containers so that you can quickly and easily see the color you require.

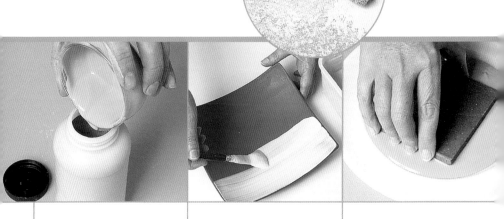

Storing

Store your slips in airtight containers to prevent the water from evaporating and thickening the slip. Try to keep the containers clean and free from dried clay, otherwise small fragments may fall into the slip and create lumps. The slip will settle in the container, and the layer of water can be poured off to thicken a slip, or stirred back in to retain a thinner consistency. Label your jars clearly.

Brushing and sponging slip

Brush the slip onto the surface of your tile in even strokes with a soft brush. It may be necessary to apply several coats to cover a dark clay body. Allow each coat to touch dry before applying the next.

Natural sponges are best used for this method. Apply several layers, allowing each to dry before applying the next. Open textured sponges create great effects when applying different colors where one is visible below another.

Dipping

The quickest way to apply a base coat of slip to a tile is to dip it. The tile should be leather hard for easy handling. Pour the slip into a saucer and immerse the surface of the tile into it, ensuring that it is evenly coated. Allow the surface to dry to the touch-dry stage before further decoration.

Creating a design
This section builds on from the last by showing how slip can be used in many different ways and combinations to create unique designs.

PAPER RESIST
This is a method of decorating which uses paper shapes to create a pattern or design on the surface of a tile—in much the same way as a stencil. The paper acts as a resist when colored slip is applied over the surface, leaving the design in sharp outline when removed.

Tip
If you leave a small area of each paper shape exposed, you will easily be able to see them later when it is time to remove them.

Making a paper resist
1 Cut shapes from newspaper for the design on the surface of your tile. Dip the shapes in water before applying them to the surface of the tile. Make sure the shapes are sealed down; if necessary, paint on a little water and brush them flat.

2 Carefully sponge a colored slip over the entire surface, including the paper shapes. Be careful not to lift the shapes as you sponge. Allow the surface to dry off to the touch.

3 Using an open-textured natural sponge, apply a light third coat of colored slip to the surface of the tile, allowing the color underneath to show through.

Sponging slip onto the surface of a tile is a method of slip application that can be used to build up a flat layer of color, or to create a multicolored effect as shown here.

4 When the surface of the tile has dried to the touch, remove the paper cutouts. Use a potter's pin to avoid digging into the surface.

You could decorate the surface further with sgraffito (see page 35) in the resist areas but there is always a danger of overworking a design. Sometimes less is more!

PAPER STENCILS

Paper stencils are an extension of the paper resist technique, except that the negative rather than positive section is used, so that the slip is applied through the cut-out paper rather than around it.

SLIP TRAILING

This is not an easy technique to master, so practice on newspaper until you feel confident enough to try on a tile. Don't despair if you get it wrong—you can always scrape the slip off while it's still wet and try again.

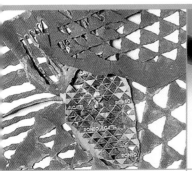

Paper stencils

This series of stencils cut from thick absorbent paper will make interesting shapes and patterns when used as resists for slip. This type of paper can be washed and reused many times. You can also use newspaper, but then the stencil can only be used once.

Slip trailing

Fill your slip-trailing bulb with fairly thick slip about the consistency of whipped cream. Squeeze the bulb in a consistent action as you draw out your design; this helps avoid spattering. Using both hands sometimes helps steady the technique. You may find it helpful to practice on sheets of paper until you are confident enough to work on clay.

Slip inlay

1 Here, an incised pattern has been drawn onto a leather-hard surface. A contrasting colored slip is then painted into the lines, as thickly as possible.

The slip may shrink as it dries, requiring another coat to build it up to the surface level.

2 When the inlay has dried to the leather-hard stage, carefully scrape away the excess slip with a metal kidney or scraper to reveal the inlaid pattern underneath.

INLAY

Inlaying is a versatile method of embedding contrasting colored clays into the surface of a tile. You will need patience and a steady hand to perfect this technique successfully. The hardest part of this technique is judging when to scrape away the excess slip or clay, but once you have mastered it, you will find that there is something very satisfying in seeing the linear design emerge from under the slip.

Soft clay inlay

The center of this tile is being decorated with lines of porcelain clay. Use a metal scraper in the same way as for inlay to remove excess clay and reveal the motif underneath.

Sgraffito

Sgraffito is a form of incising or drawing into clay. The technique is usually used on surfaces with a contrasting slip to the clay body so that when you cut through the slip the clay color is revealed.

Marbling slip

Pour areas of contrasting colored slips onto a tile. Shake the tile to move the colors around to form variegated patterns that look like marble. Don't shake the tile for too long, or the colors will merge and look muddy. Carefully pour away any excess and wipe the edge clean.

Tube-line mix

The mix must have three things: clay to bind it together, a flux to fuse the line onto the tile, and a granular material such as quartz to reduce its contraction on firing.

The following recipe is suitable if a commercially made mix is not available. The percentages given are by weight.

- 36% china clay
- 36% quartz
- 16% ball clay
- 4% whiting
- 4% standard borax frit
- 4% high alkaline frit

Combine the materials with water, initially making the mix thin so it can be pushed through a very fine strainer. Let it stand for 24 hours, after which time some water will have separated out and can be skimmed off. It then needs to thicken further, so place it in an open container in a warm room to encourage evaporation.

Tube lining on biscuit-fired tiles

1 Transfer the design to a biscuit-fired tile with a smooth, even surface.

2 Fill a fine-nozzled (1 mm diameter) slip trailer with the tube-line mix (see above). Shake the bottle well. If the mix is too thin, it will flow out too freely. To produce a fine continuous line, keep the tip of the nozzle in contact with the tile. Work by drawing the bottle toward you, which keeps the lines smoother.

3 Fine details that are to appear as texture beneath the glazes (rather than as boundaries between them) can be painted on with the tube-line mix, using a brush.

4 When dry, fill in the areas of the design with colored glazes. Flood these onto the surface of the tile using a slip trailer with a wider nozzle than that used for the lining mix. Make their consistency the same as a brush-on glaze (see page 41). The thinner the glazes, the more care must be taken with their application. Start with the thinnest and let each dry before applying the next. Always wear protective gloves when handling glazes.

Textured surfaces
Texturing the surface of clay is an exciting yet simple way of making unique tiles.

This is a method of decorating whereby textured materials are rolled into the clay to form a design or pattern. Embossed wallpaper is particularly good for this technique because it is available in such a vast range of designs and can be cut to any shape, but organic materials also make wonderful impressions in clay and are readily available to all—even weeds work!

Drying tiles
Dry the completed tiles slowly, to prevent warping or curling. It is essential that the tiles dry evenly— warping is often caused by drying on one side. Lay the tiles on wire racks to allow air to pass under them. Open-mesh baking trays for cakes are good and inexpensive, but be sure not to use them again for baking afterward. You can also turn your tiles regularly during drying, or dry them slowly between wooden boards.

Wallpapers
Embossed wallpapers make similar impressions in clay to fabrics, but they have the added advantage that you can cut out shapes to form repeats if you want to create a particular effect.

Decorating stores often allow their customers to take away samples of paper, so try a few before buying a whole roll. Lay the paper on your slab with the roller guides still in place at each side. Roll over it carefully but firmly. Lift a corner of the paper with a pin to remove it.

Organic material
Try rolling leaves into the surface of the clay. Choose ones with interesting shapes or outlines, and preferably with distinct veining on the underside to make a good impression in the clay. Deciduous leaves are best because they are soft, but conifers can also make good marks. Some flowers work well, but try seedheads, bark, and seaweed as well.

Glazing—methods of application

Glaze is the glass-like surface that gives tiles their shiny finish. Glazes are made from various rocks and minerals, ground down into powders and combined in various quantities to give specific effects

TYPES AND MIXING

The main constituents of a glaze are silica (the glass former), alumina (this makes the glaze stiff, to stop it running off when being fired), and a flux that controls the melting temperature. Further materials can be added in small percentages to give color and other effects. Glazes can have shiny, satin, or matte finishes, and can be transparent or opaque, white or colored.

Mixing glazes

1 Weigh out the dry ingredients into a bowl and gently mix them together, trying not to create much dust. Always wear a mask when dry-mixing powders, both when formulating your own glazes and when you use commercially prepared glaze powder.

2 When all the particles are fully mixed, begin to slowly add them to the water. Add them gradually, sprinkling the mix onto the surface of the water so you don't make any lumps.

3 When all the glaze powder has been added, stir the mixture thoroughly, breaking up any large particles between your fingers.

It is possible to formulate and mix your own glazes. Alternatively, you may prefer to buy glazes ready-mixed from your pottery supplier. They are available in powder form or ready to use in buckets; some are applied by brushing.

Commercially prepared transparent glazes can be colored by the addition of metal oxides in small quantities, or by slightly larger percentages of ready-mixed glaze stains or underglaze colors. If you intend to combine different color glazes on the same tile, using the same base glaze with different colors added will ensure that each glaze is compatible and should not create problems in firing.

When adding water to glaze, use a ratio of 2 lb 3 oz (1 kg) of dry glaze powder to between 2 ½ and 3 pints (1 and 1.4 liters) of water. This is only a guide, because the thickness of glaze you require for a particular application will vary.

4 Rest a strainer on two sticks over another bowl, and pour in the stirred mixture. If the mix is thick at this stage, you will have to add more water. Don't add too much at once, in case you make the mix too thin.

5 Many potters use a "lawn brush," a stiff, long-bristled brush, to stir the mix through the strainer. A good alternative is to use a stiff rubber kidney; this helps to push a thicker mix through the strainer, and is easier to clean afterward.

6 Another alternative is to use a nail brush. The short, hard bristles force the liquid through the strainer. The size of the holes in the sieve is important, the best thing being about 80-mesh, but if you intend to spray glazes, the mesh will need to be finer.

COLORING AND APPLYING GLAZES

When mixing colorants into glaze, make only small amounts to begin with—this avoids the disappointment of mixing a huge bucket of glaze only to find that you do not like the color when you test it. It is essential to keep accurate records of each of your tests so that the recipe can be repeated—this will include noting the detail on the back of the sample using an oxide wash that will not stick to the kiln shelf when fired.

Coloring glazes

1 Coloring commercial glazes is an easy way to make your own colors. Add about 10 percent of bought underglaze colors or body/glaze stains (dry weight) to a small amount of water, and mix thoroughly to a milky consistency.

2 Add the dry glaze powder to the bowl of water, and mix thoroughly before pouring into the watered colorants. Stir the two mixes together before straining them through a 120-mesh strainer. The strainer must be finer than the previous example to be sure that all the fine color is evenly distributed through the glaze.

3 Always test all your glazes before applying them to tiles. Many disappointments occur when the glaze is not what you expect or has been applied too thinly, and your hard work and effort has been ruined. Cut a series of small slabs and biscuit-fire them, afterward applying the glaze and refiring. Keep these tiles as reminders.

Tip

Use a damp sponge to thoroughly wipe away any glaze from the surface on which the tile will sit in the kiln—otherwise your tile will seal onto the kiln shelf.

DIPPING

The most convenient technique for applying a glaze to tiles is dipping. This relies on the ability of a biscuit-fired clay body to absorb water. The tile is immersed in a bowl of glaze in a single smooth motion and held submerged while water enters the body, leaving a layer of glaze adhering to the surface. When the tile is removed, it must be held with the finished surface uppermost while any excess glaze drains off.

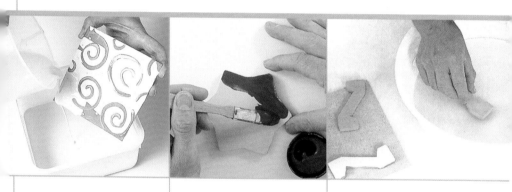

Pouring

Fill a jug or similar container with glaze. Hold your tile over the glaze bucket as you pour the glaze over the surface. Do this in one action to avoid building up different thicknesses of glaze.

Brushing

Brushing glaze onto the surface of tiles is more difficult than dipping because water from the glaze is quickly absorbed into the porous surface of the biscuit clay. However, with some practice, you will be able to master the technique.

Place your tile on a board with your glaze bucket close by. Load your brush with glaze and apply it to the surface. Repeat the process until the entire surface is covered evenly.

Dipping

If you are using a thick glaze for dipping, simply skim the finished face of the tile through the surface of the glaze and then shake the tile to even out any runs.

GLAZE APPLICATION

Tiles will stick better to adhesives and grouts if their backs and edges are unglazed. It is also necessary for firing that the underside of the tile is unglazed, otherwise it will fuse to the kiln shelf as the glaze melts in the firing process— destroying not only your tile, but the kiln shelf as well.

Dipping large tiles

When dipping a large, thick tile it is easy to hold the edges between your fingertips and still avoid leaving marks in the glaze.

Dipping frames

A small wire dipping frame is needed when you are glazing thin tiles. Just the very tip of your thumb can be used for support.

Protecting the back of tiles

To prevent unwanted glaze from adhering to the back of a tile, sponge on a thin coating of wax emulsion.

Removing excess glaze

Remove excess glaze from the edges of a tile by running a penknife or similar blade around while the glaze is still wet.

Before firing

Before placing your tile in a kiln, give it a wipe with a damp sponge to remove any final traces of glaze still sticking to the wax resist.

UNDERGLAZE COLORS APPLIED WITH SHAPED SPONGES

Underglaze colors are available in powder or liquid form; you can choose either type for this technique. If using powders, simply water down to a paint-like consistency before use. Shaped sponges are widely available from craft suppliers and some ceramic suppliers, but you can also make your own. Dampen a sponge and put it in the freezer for a while. Draw out your design on the frozen sponge, and then cut it out using a sharp craft knife.

Underglaze design is usually applied directly onto a white biscuit surface, which allows for the best color response. If you have only red clay, you can apply several layers of white slip before firing to overcome the problem. Underglaze colors can also be brushed onto the surface for a more painterly effect.

Applying underglaze colors with shaped sponges

1 Prepare your colors on a plate or old tile surface ready for use. Dampen your shaped sponge. Load the sponge with color by using a brush or simply by dipping it. The advantage of applying the color with a brush is that you can be very specific about where the different colors are placed.

2 Sponge the design onto your chosen surface using gentle but firm pressure. Think about the positioning of the pattern and carry the design over the edges if appropriate. Reload the sponge when the pattern appears to be thinning too much.

3 Add finer details in a contrasting color with a thin brush. Apply a transparent glaze over the design and fire to the required temperature.

BRUSH-ON GLAZES

A huge range of commercially prepared glazes is available from ceramic suppliers. The range extends from very low-firing decorative finishes through to high-fired glaze suitable for domestic use. Studio potters generally do not use these glazes because they can be quite expensive and are only available in relatively small containers. However, because you only need to purchase the smallest amounts, the beginner may find it interesting to try them.

MAJOLICA

Majolica is the term used to describe the technique of painting colors over an unfired dry glaze surface. When fired, the colors melt into the glaze to fuse the design, which explains the technique's other name: in-glaze decoration.

Generally a white tin glaze is used as the base, although traditionally a transparent glaze would be applied over a white slip body. You could try both methods to see how they differ.

When tin glaze is used over red earthenware clay, the result is commonly referred to as tin-glaze earthenware.

Applying brush-on glaze

Simply choose your glazes from the ceramic catalog and paint them onto your tiles following the manufacturer's instructions. Several coats of glaze are usually required for a satisfactory result.

Majolica

Mix powdered underglaze colors with a small amount of glaze and a few drops of water to a paint-like consistency. Glaze your surface with white tin glaze and allow to dry.

Apply large areas of color with a soft bristle brush. Load the brush with color to avoid running out mid-stroke because mistakes will show up in the firing. Build up the design using more colors and different sized brushes for finer detail.

Glazing using paper stencils

Paper or card stencils make a good resist for clearly defined patterns. They can be used for glaze-on-glaze techniques or as an extension of the majolica technique.

The stencil should be slightly larger than the tile so that it can be taped to either side of the tile to secure it in place.

Spattering glaze or oxide with an old toothbrush is another interesting way of applying secondary treatments to a pre-glazed surface.

Glazing decoration

Glazing need not be an end in itself—there are many ways of using glaze creatively with the use of a few extra materials.

OXIDE DECORATION

Metal oxides are a traditional method of applying decoration to biscuit-fired tiles and can be used in several ways.

Safety note

Because of their toxic nature, oxides should not come into direct contact with skin. Wear rubber gloves to protect yourself.

Oxide on textured surface

Oxide can be used as a finish in its own right without the covering of glaze; it gives a rustic effect that is often suited to pieces for the outdoors or the yard. It is particularly good on texture, as it brings out the detail in the surface.

1 In this example, water is added to red iron oxide to form a thick emulsion. Paint the oxide onto the clay surface, making sure that all the texture detail is filled in.

2 Wear rubber gloves to sponge the oxide carefully away from the surface, but leave it in the texture patterning to sharply define the detail. The oxide will stay in all surface marks to add interest to the finished work.

Painted oxide on glaze

Oxide can be painted directly onto a glazed surface, but this requires a slightly freer hand because the powdery glaze absorbs the oxide mixture very quickly, making it difficult to draw the brush across the surface.

A simple white tin glaze is used in this example, with cobalt oxide forming the decoration.

PAINTED OXIDE ON BISCUIT CLAY

Oxides can be used like paints to draw designs onto biscuit-fired clay surfaces. This example shows a fine pattern of cobalt oxide being painted onto a tile, which will later be covered with a transparent or opaque glaze to soften the effect.

WAX RESIST

Wax for resist techniques can be bought in emulsion form from ceramic suppliers and applied with a paintbrush. Wash your brushes in very hot water after use to remove all the wax.

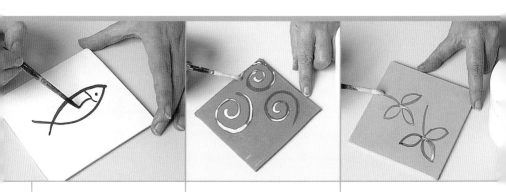

Applying oxides

Mix the oxide with a little water to achieve a thin consistency for painting. Use a fine brush to paint oxides and try not to be too careful in the way you apply it. Be aware that cobalt oxide is quite strong, so a little will cover a large area. It need not be as thick as the last example (painted oxide on glaze); a simple wash will give good results.

Wax resist under glaze

Wax resist under glaze is a simple but effective technique that allows a pattern to be painted onto a biscuit-fired surface, which prevents the glaze from being absorbed when applied. When the tile is fired, the wax burns away and the matte clay body color is left in contrast to the shiny glaze (although you could equally well apply a dry firing glaze for effect).

Wax resist over glaze

The principle for this technique is almost the same as for the last, but the pattern is painted over a pre-glazed surface so that the base glaze color will show through when subsequent glazes are applied over the top.

1 Begin by glazing your tile in a color of your choice, and then paint your design in wax emulsion over the top.

Tips

• You can use liquid latex instead of wax, with the added benefit that each layer can be removed after glaze application. This allows you to see more clearly how the design is building up.
• If you use latex, be sure to wash your brushes in boiling water after use; otherwise they will be ruined. A little detergent in the water also helps.

2 When the wax is dry, sponge another, contrasting glaze over the pattern to block out the base glaze color.

3 Apply some secondary wax detail to the surface to further enhance the finish.

4 Complete the surface by sponging a final coat of glaze in yet another color on selected areas to correspond with the last wax detail.

Post-glaze decoration
Enamels and luster are applied onto a fired glazed surface. This could be one of your own tiles but it is possible to fire them onto commercially glazed tiles if you prefer.

ENAMELS

Enamels are prepared colors composed of metal oxides and fluxes that are applied to previously fired glazes, and which melt at low temperatures to fuse onto the surface. The firing range for enamels is similar to luster, but starts at around 1,202–1,400°F (650–780°C).

Enamels are the brightest of all ceramic colorants and are available from ceramic suppliers in a wide range of hues in either liquid or powder form. If you buy the powder variety, you will also need to purchase a special oil medium to mix the color for application.

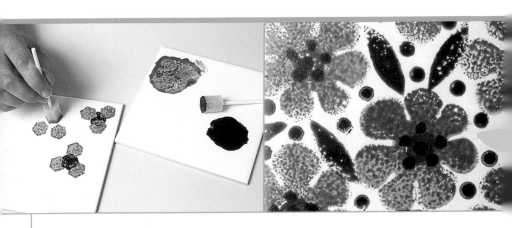

Applying enamels

You can apply enamels with a brush or a sponge. In this example, small shaped sponges are used to build up a design. The enamel colors have been prepared on a tile in advance to make the application by sponge easier.

If you make a mistake when applying the enamel, simply wipe it off and begin again. The firing of enamels must be slow at first to allow the oil medium to burn off. If you fire the enamel too quickly, the oil will boil and cause bubbling on the surface of the tile which will ruin the finish.

Safety note

It is important to ventilate your room well when applying and firing luster.

LUSTER

Precious metal luster is quite an expensive treatment for clay and requires some practice to apply. Luster colors are not quite so expensive and can be used for experimenting.

Luster is usually used to highlight certain details on a ceramic surface as a final detail when the work has gone through all firing procedures. It can be applied over glaze for a shiny, lustrous effect or directly onto the fired clay body for a more subtle, matte finish.

The luster is usually fired at 1,292–1,400°F (700–780°C); any higher and it will simply burn off.

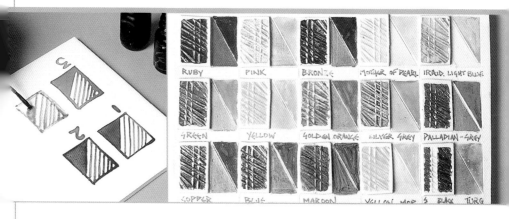

Applying luster

1 Luster is sticky to apply and all colors are brown before firing, which can be confusing. To overcome this, apply only one color to all relevant areas at a time. Paint the luster thinly but evenly in the required areas directly from the file container. Clean the brush after each use in luster thinner (a liquid developed for thinning luster when it has become too thick) to avoid contaminating the colors.

2 If you intend to use lusters regularly, it is a good idea to make a test tile of all the colors to show how they look on different surfaces.

This tile shows the range of luster colors on a glazed surface in its shiny form, on an unglazed surface for the matte form, and on texture for a quite different finish. The color of each luster is written underneath each sample for quick reference.

Simple printing methods Here are a few methods of marking your design directly onto a tile, either with color or with texture.

MONOPRINTING

Monoprinting is a direct and simple way of transferring drawn images onto a raw clay surface while still retaining the spontaneity of the sketch. The process involves painting oxides onto a board and allowing them to dry. You then draw the desired image onto a piece of paper placed on top of the oxide-covered board. The oxides adhere to the reverse side of the image and this can then be transferred onto clay. In the example shown below, a freely drawn portrait is transferred onto a slab of porcelain for a wall tile. You can also reproduce images onto the sides of pots in this way.

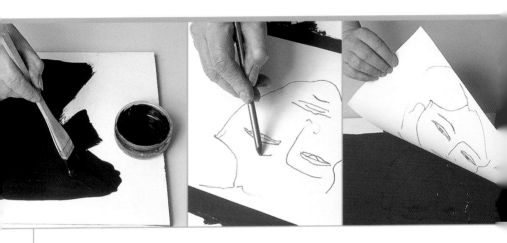

Single color printing

1 Paint an even layer of thick oxide on the face of a smooth melamine-covered board. Allow the oxide to dry thoroughly. You can use a hot-air gun to speed up the process if you wish. The board must have a nonabsorbent surface so that the dry oxide will lift off onto the paper.

2 Place a sheet of paper onto the dry oxide and draw the image on the paper with a pencil or tool. Make sure you hold the paper down firmly so that it does not move while you draw.

3 Carefully peel off the paper, removing it cleanly from the oxide to avoid smudging the image. You will be able to see the clear lines of oxide on the reverse side of the drawing.

USING OXIDES

Using a variety of painted oxides, the whole range of colors becomes possible. You can paint different colored oxides onto different areas of the board to change the color of the drawn line that will be applied to the clay. A variety of tools can be used to create a range of marks and rubbing with your finger will give softer areas of color. After the initial image has been transferred, you can work into the surface of the clay with additional oxides, slips, stains, or impressed textures. Be inventive and experiment with the technique, combining other decorating methods to achieve highly individual results.

INTAGLIO PRINTING

Intaglio is a printmaking term, from the Italian word intaglione, meaning to engrave or cut. In ceramics it refers to the technique of cutting an image into a block and transferring it to a clay surface. The most common method is to carve a design into a slab of plaster and press clay firmly onto the image

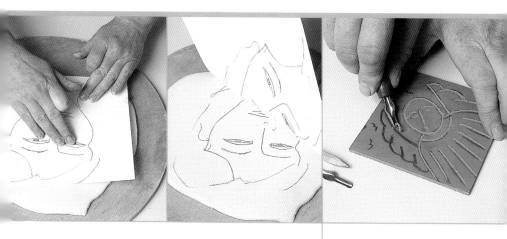

4 Place the paper oxide-side down onto the damp surface of a clay slab and rub your fingers over the paper. The oxide powder will stick to the damp clay beneath.

5 Peel off the paper to reveal the transfer print. At this stage, you could paint the image with oxides or slips or leave it as a line drawing.

Cutting a lino block

Draw your design onto a printer's lino block in pencil or ink (ordinary vinyl flooring will also work well, but it cannot be cut as deeply). Use lino-cutting tools to engrave the design into the surface, following your drawn lines.

so that it is transferred to the clay. However, a more versatile method is to cut the design into a block of linoleum, which can then be pressed into the clay. Working in this way can give highly distinctive and accurate repeat images, ideal for creating a series of plates or tiles. The raised lines of intaglio printing produce wonderful patterns for borders, simple repeat motifs, and intricate drawn designs. After biscuit firing, underglaze colors, stains, or oxides can be painted onto the surface.

Printing and coloring

1 Lay the lino block onto a slab of soft clay, and firmly roll over it so that the image is transferred successfully. Lift off the block and inspect the image. If further detail is needed, you can cut into the block a little deeper. The impressed clay slab can then be formed into dishes, pots, or left as tiles.

2 After biscuit firing to 1,830°F (1,000°C), paint the design with your chosen colors. Here, underglaze colors are mixed with plain water and painted onto the surface. When using commercial stains such as these, you can see the hues and tones build up, but you could use oxides for richer colors if you prefer.

3 When dry, lightly rub off some of the color with your finger to create a more subtle effect. Deeper shades will build up around the raised lines, emphasizing the decoration. Fire to a higher temperature to bring out the full intensity of the colors.

Transferring motifs

There are several ways of transferring motifs or designs to the surface of a tile, but the one you choose will depend very much on the technique to be used for decoration. In many cases it will be sufficient to copy the design onto paper which can then be positioned directly over the tile and the pattern transferred by tracing over the lines with a sharp pencil.

Tracing

When the pattern is complete, roll out a slab of smooth clay, using roller guides no thicker than 2 in. (5 cm). Carefully cut out a 6-in. (15-cm) square from the slab and transfer it to a nonabsorbent board that is at least 2 in. (5 cm) larger. Ensure that the slab sticks to the surface well and that the edges have a slight inward bevel to avoid undercuts. Place a paper design over the clay square and transfer the pattern by tracing over the lines.

Using a "spons"

For reproducing large or complicated designs you can create a "spons." Copy the pattern on good-quality tracing paper, then pierce a series of holes along every line with a compass point or a large-gauge needle. Hold the spons over the tile and pounce finely-ground charcoal powder through the holes with a soft brush.

Using transfer paper

Transfer paper is invaluable for copying intricate detail, and it is available from most good artists' supply stores. From Delftware to William Morris designs, any image can be transferred.

Transfer paper is a thin tissue paper with graphite backing. Place it under a design and trace over to deliver an identical line of graphite, durable enough to withstand smudging, but removable with a damp cotton swab. Carbon paper can also be used.

Decorating commercially made tiles

A wall of plain tiles offers a wonderful canvas for decoration, and the diversity of paint is limitless.

Paint can be applied in a number of ways; obviously by paint brush, but the finish can be uninteresting. However, by contrast, stipple brushes designed for use with stencils can create wonderful textured effects. Similarly, sponges can create very subtle or textured finishes and both natural and synthetic versions can be used.

Toothbrushes are useful to create spattered effects and even crumpled fabrics or plastic bags will give exciting results. Experiment first on spare tiles to see which effect you prefer!

BEFORE GETTING STARTED

Before you start to decorate your tiles, they must be free of finger prints and dust so wipe them down with a surface cleaner.

Allow adequate ventilation when spraying lacquer or using enamel paint as the fumes are extremely toxic and highly flammable. A build up of these fumes could be dangerous.

Always work in a clean and dry environment— this type of tile decoration is non-utilitarian—so you should be aware that neither lacquer nor varnish will give protection against persistent damp or abrasion. You will need to decide carefully which tiles you want to decorate in specific areas.

TYPES OF PAINT

As glazed tiles are nonabsorbent, more durable paints such as enamel or acrylic are most suitable; however, these will need to be sealed with lacquer or varnish to be durable. There are now a good range of paints available which are designed especially for use on tiles and which do not need sealing after application, so look in your hardware store for these.

Enamels

Acrylics

Varnish

Tile paints

APPLICATION WHEN USING STENCILS

There are two main methods of applying paint when stenciling; the first involves the use of a special stippling brush. These are available from any good craft supplier, though they are relatively expensive. A good and inexpensive alternative is to use sponges—the synthetic kind are perfectly acceptable and one large sponge can be cut up into manageable sizes for use with different paint colors, unlike a brush, which will need to be cleaned each time you want to change the color.

If acrylic or enamel paints are used to decorate your tiles, you will need to seal the surface after application to make it durable. Use gloss lacquer, clear varnish, or the sealant that is recommended by the manufacturer of the paint.

Stippling
Apply the paint by dabbing in regular movements over the area to be covered. To avoid runs, make sure the consistency of the paint is not too thin.

Sponging
Use a small piece of sponge for easier handling. Dab the paint on evenly while working the sponge gently to avoid paint squeezing out and underneath the stencil edges.

Paint can also be brushed on, but this method has a greater tendency to gather at the edges of the stencil and seep underneath so the first two methods are preferable.

You can use an ordinary paint brush in a stippling action if all else fails.

Sealing
Check that the tiles are free from fingerprints and dust, and spray from left to right with acrylic lacquer. Wait for a couple of minutes before applying another coat, to avoid making drip marks. Let it dry.

Use the sealant that is recommended for the type of paint that you have used.

MAKING STENCILS

Card stencils are simple and cheap to make, and you can use them to decorate a wall or panel of tiles.

Equipment and materials

Ruler
Pencil
Tracing paper
Cutting mat
Craft knife
Pictures of seashore objects
Masking tape
Paper
Stencil card
Spray-on glue
Sponges
Acrylic paint (in color of choice)
Spray-on clear gloss lacquer

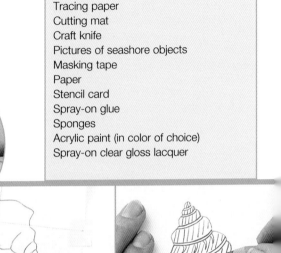

Making a stencil

1 Measure your tile and with a pencil draw it to size on a piece of tracing paper. Cut it out on a cutting mat, using a craft knife and a ruler. Draw a line down the middle and across the center to make four equal squares.

2 Position your chosen image near the center of the square and accurately trace as much detail as possible.

3 Tape the tracing onto some blank paper. If you use very thin paper, put something soft underneath such as a piece of cardboard or an old magazine. Mark the corners of the tile on the paper so you will know if the tracing has moved and where to cut the tile perimeter. Retrace the image, pressing hard with your pencil.

4 Remove the tracing and fill in the lines of the imprint on the paper. If the lines are too faint, shade in the area using the side of your pencil. This tracing technique allows for your imagination to exaggerate curves and simplify detail.

USING STENCILS

Spray the back of the stencil with a little glue to stop it from slipping and position it against a tile. Using a small piece of sponge or stencil brush, dab on the paint. Work the sponge gently to avoid paint squeezing out and running underneath the stencil edges.

After painting, remove the stencil directly away from the tile to avoid smudging. Make sure there is no paint on the reverse side of the stencil that will mark the next tile, and continue working along a row of tiles. Check each time that the stencil is straight and the image well centered.

When the paint is dry, make sure the surrounding tiles are clean and free from dust, and spray with lacquer. Wait for a couple of minutes before applying another coat, to avoid making drip marks. Leave to dry overnight, keeping the area dust-free.

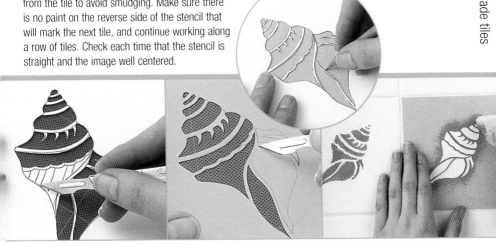

5 Divide your drawing into positive and negative parts. The positive parts are the areas of your design that will be painted and the negative areas are those that will be left blank. If an area is to be blank it will remain covered, therefore the parts of the stencil to be left intact are these negative areas. Cut out the positive shapes. Every now and again, stop to check the shapes you are making by holding the paper against a colored surface.

6 When you are satisfied with your design, place it over a piece of stencil card. Mark the corners and cut to your tile size. Tape the drawing in position on the card and draw around the inside edge of the template using a sharp pencil.

7 Remove the drawing and, using a sharp craft knife, carefully cut out the shape. Rotate your stencil as you work so your cutting action is always in the same direction.

8 Spray the back of the stencil so that it is tacky, and position it against the tile. Use a small piece of sponge to dab on the paint. Be sure to lift the stencil off carefully, so as not to smudge the lines.

DESIGN & MOTIF
DIRECTORY

Tile selector

1 Snail

2 Scorpions

3 Old-English hare

4 Tree frog

5 Snake

6 Lizard

7 Pink elephant

8 Delft-style deer

9 Cats on a wall

10 Art Deco running deer

11 Stylized bird

12 Art Deco-style bird

13 Little birds

14 Naive bird

15 Avocet

16 Framed bird

17 Monty

18 Magpie

19 Goose

20 Chicken

21 Cockerel

22 Stenciled bird

23 Birds in flight

24 Silver fish

25 Leaping fish

26 Butterfly fish

27 Jellyfish

28 Stenciled fish

29 Clown triggerfish

30 Angel fish

31 Rustic fish

32 Pink fish

33 Seahorse and shells

34 Majolica butterfly

35 Bumblebee

36 Simple repeating butterfly

37 Black-and-white butterfly

38 Fly

39 Black-and-white butterfly no. 2

40 Butterfly-wing stencil

41 Dragonfly

42 Stylized butterfly panel

43 Butterfly ring

44 Octopus

45 Crab

46 Lobster

47 Starfish on sand

48 Nautilus shell

49 Shells

50 Hydrozoan

51 Coral

 52 Yacht

 53 Stenciled shells

 54 Fossilized coral

 55 Fern

 56 Fossil fish

 57 Shells and ammonites

 58 Ammonite group

 59 Starfish fossil

 60 Large ammonite

 61 Sea urchin

 62 Aquilegia vulgaris

 63 Tulip pattern

 64 Stylized leaf design

 65 Allium seedhead

 66 Potted tree

 67 Old English tile

 68 Leaf vine

 69 Woodland floor

 70 Foliage

 71 Wallpaper texture flower

 72 Single impressed leaf

 73 Tube-lined tulip

 74 Sponged leaf design

 75 Grasses and leaves

 76 Honeysuckle

 77 Umbellifer

 78 Stenciled peony

 79 Sponged flower

 80 Papaver

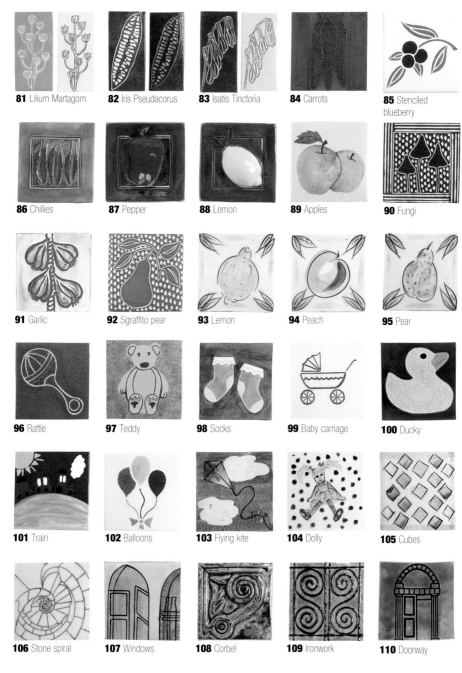

81 Lilium Martagom

82 Iris Pseudacorus

83 Isatis Tinctoria

84 Carrots

85 Stenciled blueberry

86 Chillies

87 Pepper

88 Lemon

89 Apples

90 Fungi

91 Garlic

92 Sgraffito pear

93 Lemon

94 Peach

95 Pear

96 Rattle

97 Teddy

98 Socks

99 Baby carriage

100 Ducky

101 Train

102 Balloons

103 Flying kite

104 Dolly

105 Cubes

106 Stone spiral

107 Windows

108 Corbel

109 Ironwork

110 Doorway

111 Columns

112 Castle

113 Grid plan

114 Church windows

115 Dome

116 Garden urn

117 Stonework

118 Church

119 Minaret

120 Aztec serpent

121 Greek pattern

122 Greek pattern border

123 North American Indian face

124 Buddha

125 Indian textile

126 Indian border

127 New Guinea bark cloth

128 Scandinavian rock painting

129 Egyptian scarab and lotus

130 Aboriginal stone drawing

131 Flowers

132 Water, hills, and trees

133 Abstract block

134 Flow

135 Spiral and dots

136 Diamond

137 Chim's pattern

138 Circles and squares

139 Rain

140 Seaweed

141 Swirl

142 Map

143 Hundertwasser: Windows

144 Hundertwasser: Psychedelic

145 Hundertwasser: Circles

146 Hundertwasser: Minaret crowns

147 Klee: Color grid

148 Klee: Abstract plant

149 Klee: Flowers and water

150 Klee: Stenciled plants

151 Kandinsky: Hands

152 Kandinsky: Abstract

153 Kandinsky: Shapes

154 Modigliani: Figure

155 Picasso: Profile

156 Picasso: Face

157 Libra

158 Gemini

159 Saggitarius

160 Pisces

161 Leo

162 Capricorn

163 Virgo

164 Scorpio

165 Cancer

166 Taurus

167 Aries

168 Aquarius

169 Circle knot

170 Linocut knotwork design

171 Linocut knotwork design border

172 Zoomorphic motif with knot

173 Key pattern

174 Knot cross

175 Stencil knot

176 Key pattern No. 2

177 Key pattern: Cross border

178 1950s low relief

179 1950s still life

180 1950s surface pattern

181 1950s Abstract

182 1960s flower

183 1960s hearts

184 1960s lines and circles

185 1960s psychedelic

186 1960s psychedelic border

187 1970s trees

188 1970s surface pattern

189 1970s flower

190 1970s corner pattern

191 Hexagonal snowflake

192 Hexagonal star

193 Hexagonal bolt

194 Hexagonal knot

195 Geometric lino relief

196 Curvate geometric

197 Geometric block

198 Curvate fans

199 Diamonds and circles

200 Geometric paper cut

MOTIF

Snail The combination of the majolica technique and wax resist works especially well for this simple but charming snail motif.

CLAY Red earthenware fired to 2,012°F (1,100°C) biscuit and 1,976°F (1,080°C) glaze

Order of work

1 Transfer the motif to the surface of a biscuit-fired tile.

2 Using a fine paintbrush, paint the outline detail of the snail and the border with wax emulsion.

3 Apply a coat of white tin glaze to the tile.

4 Paint over the shell and body of the snail with a selection of underglaze stains before firing to the appropriate glaze temperature.

You will need
- Red earthenware clay
- Fine paintbrush
- Wax emulsion
- White tin glaze
- Paintbrushes
- Underglaze stains

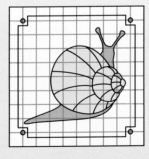

Arranging tiles
This tile can be used either as a feature or repeated as a border or frame.

DESIGN IDEAS

TECHNIQUE

DIFFICULTY

see also kilns and firing **18–21** drying tiles **37** wax resist **46** transferring motifs **53**

MOTIF

2

Scorpions

This is one of the easiest tiles to make in the book, with its stylized depiction of scorpions. The background slip color could easily be changed if you wanted to duplicate the design to add extra interest.

CLAY Red earthenware fired to 2,012°F (1,100°C) biscuit and 1,976°F (1,080°C) glaze

Order of work

1 Prepare the tile and cover with a thick coat of yellow slip.

2 When the tile has dried to the leather-hard stage, transfer the design to the surface.

3 Carefully sgraffito the outline of the design with a finely pointed tool.

4 After biscuit firing, apply a coat of transparent glaze and fire to the required temperature.

You will need

- Red earthenware clay
- Yellow slip
- Paintbrushes
- Sgraffito tool
- Transparent earthenware glaze

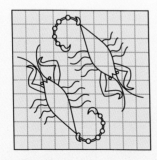

Arranging tiles

Use this tile either as a random feature mixed with other tiles of a similar style, or as a repeat in different colorways.

DESIGN IDEAS

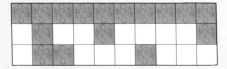

TECHNIQUE

DIFFICULTY

see also kilns and firing **18–21** applying slip **32** drying tiles **37** transferring motifs **53**

MOTIF

Old English Hare This tile is a copy of
a medieval encaustic tile and uses two different colored clays with the same firing temperature; one to form the background, the other as inlay.

CLAY Red and white earthenware fired to 2,012°F (1,100°C) biscuit and 1,976°F (1,080°C) glaze

Order of work

1 Prepare the tile in red earthenware clay and allow to dry out to the leather-hard stage.

2 Transfer the design to the surface of the tile.

3 Carefully carve out the detail of the motif to a minimum depth of ⅛ in. (3 mm).

4 Fill in the carved-out detail with white earthenware clay, trying not to contaminate it with the red clay, then scrape it back to reveal the design.

5 After biscuit firing, cover with transparent glaze and fire to the appropriate temperature.

You will need
- Red and white earthenware clay
- Carving tool
- Transparent earthenware glaze

Arranging tiles
These tiles were traditionally used for floors, but would make an interesting addition, with others of a similar rustic style, randomly positioned in a country kitchen.

DESIGN IDEA

TECHNIQUE

DIFFICULTY

see also kilns and firing **18–21** drying tiles **37** transferring motifs **53**

MOTIF

Tree Frog
Tree frogs are such cute little creatures, and they make great motifs that look especially delightful in a child's bedroom or bathroom.

Animals

Order of work

1 Prepare the tile and allow to dry to the leather-hard stage.

2 Transfer the design to the surface of the tile and carefully incise the detail of the motif.

3 After biscuit firing, paint on a selection of colored glazes and fire to the recommended temperature.

CLAY White earthenware fired to 2,012°F (1,100°C) biscuit and 1,868°F (1,020°C) glaze

You will need
- White earthenware clay
- Incising tools
- Selection of commercial paint-on glazes
- Paintbrushes

Arranging tiles
These tiles look really good as a border or frame for plain tiles in a similar color.

DESIGN IDEA

TECHNIQUE

DIFFICULTY

see also kilns and firing **18–21** drying tiles **37** transferring motifs **53**

MOTIF

Snake This simple motif is adapted from an ethnic African textile design, and is both quick and easy to reproduce.

Order of work

1 Prepare the tile and apply a thick coat of white slip.

2 When the tile is leather hard, transfer the design to the surface and sgraffito the outline of the motif.

3 After biscuit firing, apply a transparent glaze and fire to the recommended glaze temperature.

CLAY Red earthenware fired to 2,012°F (1,100°C) biscuit and 1,976°F (1,080°C) glaze

You will need
- Red earthenware clay
- White slip
- Paintbrushes
- Sgraffito tool
- Transparent earthenware glaze

Arranging tiles
Use this tile either as a random feature mixed with other tiles of a similar style, or as a repeat in various colorways.

DESIGN IDEA

TECHNIQUE

DIFFICULTY

1

see also kilns and firing **18–21** applying slip **32** drying tiles **37** transferring motifs **53**

MOTIF

6

Lizard
This little lizard is painted in bright colors on an unglazed terracotta background to look as though he is climbing a garden pot or wall.

Order of work

1 Transfer the design to the surface of a biscuit-fired tile.

2 Fill in the detail of the lizard with a selection of commercial paint-on colored glazes. Finish by firing to the appropriate glaze temperature.

CLAY Red earthenware fired to 2,012°F (1,100°C) biscuit and 1,976°F (1,080°C) glaze

You will need
- Red earthenware clay
- Selection of commercial paint-on glazes
- Paintbrushes

Arranging tiles
These tiles would work well in columns, set into a scheme of plain tiles, to look as though a procession of lizards is climbing up the wall.

DESIGN IDEAS

TECHNIQUE

DIFFICULTY

see also kilns and firing **18–21** applying slip **32** drying tiles **37** transferring motifs **53**

MOTIF

7

Pink Elephant Elephants are popular motifs, and this is quite a naive interpretation of this endearing animal, in a delicate pink color.

CLAY Red earthenware fired to 2,012°F (1,100°C) biscuit and 1,976°F (1,080°C) glaze

Order of work

1 Use a craft knife to cut out the elephant from a 6-in. (15-cm) square of newspaper. You will need both the negative and positive sections of paper.

2 Dampen the paper elephant and position it on a prepared leather-hard tile, then sponge on a colored slip and allow to dry off to the touch.

3 Remove the paper elephant and position the dampened paper background over the tile. Sponge over this with pink slip.

4 Remove the paper and paint in a white tusk using white slip, then sgraffito any detail to define the outlines.

5 After biscuit firing, cover with transparent glaze and fire to the glaze temperature.

You will need
- Red earthenware clay
- Selection of colored slips
- Newspaper
- Natural sponge
- Sgraffito tool
- Transparent earthenware glaze

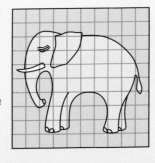

Arranging tiles
For the best results, mix this tile with plain tiles and other tiles of a similar style.

DESIGN IDEA

TECHNIQUE

DIFFICULTY

1 **2** **3**

see also kilns and firing **18–21** drying tiles **37**

MOTIF

Delft-Style Deer

This deer is painted in cobalt oxide onto a tin-glaze base, with a patterned corner detail to create a repeat. The deer itself is not in the delft style, but the pose has similarities.

CLAY Red earthenware fired to 2,012°F (1,100°C) biscuit and 1,976°F (1,080°C) glaze

Order of work

1 Apply white tin glaze to a biscuit-fired tile.

2 Transfer the design to the glazed surface.

3 Use a fine paintbrush to carefully paint in the outline detail of the motif using a thin wash of cobalt oxide. Glaze fire to the recommended temperature.

You will need

- Red earthenware clay
- White tin glaze
- Paintbrushes
- Cobalt oxide
- Fine paintbrush

Arranging tiles

The tiles form a complete repeat because of the corner patterns.

DESIGN IDEA

TECHNIQUE

DIFFICULTY

see also kilns and firing **18–21** drying tiles **37** oxide decoration **45–47** transferring motifs **53**

MOTIF

9

Cats On A Wall
Cats are extremely popular pets and therefore also make popular motifs. These cats are watching the world go by from the garden wall, or is it some kind of meeting?

CLAY White earthenware fired to 2,012°F (1,100°C) biscuit and 1,976°F (1,080°C) glaze

Order of work

1 Prepare the tile and dry to leather hard.

2 Transfer the design to the surface of the tile and sgraffito the outline detail.

3 Fill in the motif with a colored slip, then scrape back the excess slip to reveal the image below.

4 After biscuit firing, cover with transparent glaze and fire to the required temperature.

You will need
- White earthenware clay
- Colored slip
- Sgraffito tool
- Transparent earthenware glaze

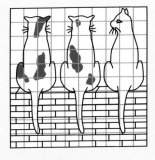

Arranging tiles
This is very much a feature tile, and would fit into a plain scheme interspersed with other images of cats made using the same technique.

DESIGN IDEA

TECHNIQUE

DIFFICULTY

see also kilns and firing **18–21** drying tiles **37** transferring motifs **53**

Art Deco Running Deer

The highly stylized image of running deer was a typical motif of the art deco period, and its sharp outlines lend themselves perfectly to this technique, and the luster finish reflects the period's opulence.

Order of work

1 Transfer the design to stencil card and carefully cut out the motif.

2 Position the stencil in place on a commercially glazed tile, using masking tape to secure it, and sponge in the detail using a thin and even application of luster.

3 When the luster has dried, fire to 1,346°F (730°C).

You will need

- Stencil card and a sharp craft knife
- Commercially glazed tile
- Masking tape
- Precious metal luster
- Natural sponge

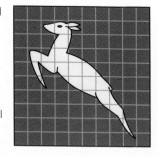

Arranging tiles

This tile works well as a border repeat with plain tiles in the same background color.

DESIGN IDEA

TECHNIQUE

DIFFICULTY

MOTIF

Stylized Bird

This funny little bird has been adapted from some designs created for a body of work some years ago. He has a witty character but is not based on any particular bird.

CLAY White earthenware fired to 2,012°F (1,100°C) biscuit and 1,868°F (1,020°C) glaze

Order of work

1 Prepare the tile and allow it to dry to leather hard.

2 Transfer the design to the tile and carefully sgraffito the outline into the clay.

3 After biscuit firing, paint the bird using paint-on glazes in the colors of your choice and fire to the recommended temperature.

You will need
- White earthenware clay
- Sgraffito tool
- Selection of commercial paint-on glazes
- Paintbrushes

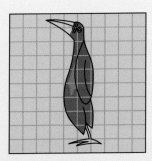

Arranging tiles
This tile looks particularly effective as a random feature, with other designs interspersed into a plain tile scheme.

DESIGN IDEA

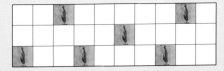

TECHNIQUE

DIFFICULTY

see also kilns and firing **18–21** drying tiles **37** transferring motifs **53**

MOTIF

Art Deco-Style Bird

This motif was adapted from an art deco tile, using a cut lino block to form an intaglio print-style finish, which is similar in effect to the tube-lined technique used at the time to create a raised outline.

Order of work

1 Transfer the design to a lino block and carefully cut it out using a range of cutting tools to create different lines and textures.

2 Prepare the tile and impress the lino block into it to transfer the design.

3 After biscuit firing, carefully paint in the detail using a range of paint-on glaze colors and fire to the required temperature.

CLAY White earthenware fired to 2,012°F (1,100°C) biscuit and 1,868°F (1,020°C) glaze

You will need
- 6-in. (15-cm) square lino block
- Lino-cutting tools
- White earthenware clay
- Selection of commercial paint-on glazes
- Paintbrushes

Arranging tiles
This style of tile could be positioned randomly in a scheme of plain tiles, or used in columns, as the Victorians did, to form a frame or border.

DESIGN IDEA

TECHNIQUE

DIFFICULTY

see also kilns and firing **18–21** drying tiles **37** transferring motifs **53**

MOTIF

Little Birds

The naive little birds on this tile were cut into small offcuts of lino blocks—providing a good way of using up the scraps—and used as stamps to impress the detail into the clay.

Order of work

1 Transfer the designs to offcuts of lino block and cut them out using a fine cutting tool that will allow you to work the intricate details.

2 Prepare the tile and sgraffito divide it into four sections.

3 Impress each linocut centrally into the four sections.

4 After biscuit firing, glaze the tile in a single color to pool in the detail, and fire to the recommended temperature.

CLAY White stoneware fired to 1,832°F (1,000°C) biscuit and 2,336°F (1,280°C) glaze

You will need
- Lino offcuts
- Fine lino-cutting tool
- White stoneware clay
- Sgraffito tool
- Stoneware glaze

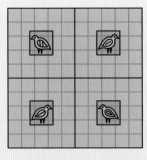

Arranging tiles
This tile could happily cover a whole wall, or be used as a random feature in a plain scheme.

DESIGN IDEA

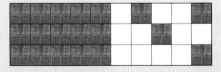

TECHNIQUE

DIFFICULTY

1 **2** **3**

see also kilns and firing **18–21** drying tiles **37**

14 Naive Bird

This motif is an almost childlike interpretation of a bird—a style that was popular in the 1950s. The sgraffito background detail is especially reminiscent of that time.

CLAY Red earthenware fired to 2,012°F (1,100°C) biscuit and 1,976°F (1,080°C) glaze

Order of work

1 Prepare the tile and apply a base slip color.

2 Cut out a newspaper bird template, dampen it, and position it centrally on the tile.

3 Use strips of paper to section off one-third of the tile, then sponge this area using two different slip colors.

4 Remove the sectioning paper strips, leaving the bird template in place, and fill in the remaining two sections in the same way, using different slip colors.

5 Remove all paper templates and sgraffito in the detail, then after biscuit-firing, apply transparent glaze and re-fire.

You will need

- Red earthenware clay
- Selection of colored slips
- Newspaper
- Natural sponge
- Sgraffito tool
- Transparent earthenware glaze

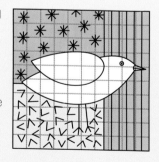

Arranging tiles

This tile would look particularly effective as a random tile among others of similar design.

DESIGN IDEA

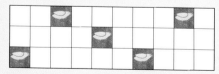

MOTIF

15

Avocet
An avocet is a wonderfully graphic, black-and-white bird that makes a sophisticated but simple motif for a tile.

CLAY Porcelain fired to 1,832°F (1,000°C) biscuit and 2,336°F (1,280°C) glaze

Order of work

1 Prepare the tile and allow to dry to the leather-hard stage.

2 Transfer the outline of the design to the tile and carefully sgraffito the outline of the bird.

3 After biscuit firing, fill in the sgraffito outline with black glaze, making sure to wipe away any excess carefully, and fire to the appropriate temperature.

You will need
- Porcelain clay
- Sgraffito tool
- Black stoneware glaze
- Paintbrush

Arranging tiles
This tile looks excellent when randomly positioned in a plain white tile scheme, perhaps with a few other tiles of a similar design.

DESIGN IDEA

TECHNIQUE

DIFFICULTY

1

see also kilns and firing **18–21** drying tiles **37** transferring motifs **53**

Framed Bird
This little bird is framed in a textured border, made by impressing embossed wallpaper into the clay, to add extra detail to the design. The frame could be left untextured if you simply want to duplicate the motif.

CLAY White stoneware fired to 1,832°F (1,000°C) biscuit and 2,336°F (1,280°C) glaze

Order of work

1 Prepare the tile and cut out a wallpaper border.

2 Position the wallpaper border over the tile, textured side down, and roll into place using roller guides, then cut the outline of the tile back to shape.

3 With the paper border still in place, transfer the outline of the bird onto the tile.

4 Sgraffito the outline of the bird and remove the wallpaper border.

5 After biscuit firing, glaze simply in a single color that will pool in the texture.

You will need
- White stoneware clay
- Textured wallpaper
- Rolling pin and roller guides
- Sgraffito tool
- Stoneware glaze

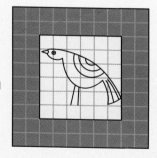

Arranging tiles
The design could be used to form a whole scheme, or be randomly positioned in a scheme of plain tiles.

DESIGN IDEAS

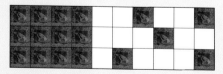

TECHNIQUE

DIFFICULTY

see also kilns and firing **18–21** drying tiles **37** transferring motifs **53**

MOTIF

17

Monty

Monty is another characterful adaptation from an early body of work, where all the designs had names to suit them.

CLAY Grogged white Raku clay fired to 1,832°F (1,000°C) biscuit and approximately 1,562–1,652°F (850–900°C) Raku glaze with a smoke reduction

Order of work

1 Prepare the tile and transfer the outline of the bird onto it, then sgraffito in the detail.

2 After biscuit firing, apply two or more Raku glazes using wax to resist any areas that are to remain unglazed, and thus be black after reduction.

3 Raku fire the tile and reduce in sawdust to achieve the blackened background.

You will need

- White Raku clay
- Sgraffito tool
- Two or more Raku glazes
- Wax emulsion
- Paintbrushes

Arranging tiles

This type of tile would look best as a feature with other tiles of a similar type, perhaps mounted and framed as an artwork.

DESIGN IDEA

TECHNIQUE

DIFFICULTY

see also kilns and firing **18–21** drying tiles **37** transferring motifs **53**

MOTIF

18

Magpie

This motif is both pictorial and graphic, in its black-and-white format, but while the composition is quite complex, the tile is actually quite easy to make.

CLAY White earthenware fired to 2,012°F (1,100°C) biscuit and 1,976°F (1,080°C) glaze

Order of work

1 Prepare the tile and apply a thick coat of black slip. Allow to dry to leather hard.

2 Transfer the design to the tile and sgraffito the outline detail.

3 Carefully incise away the areas between the trees and the white detail on the bird.

4 After biscuit firing, cover the tile with a transparent glaze and fire to the appropriate temperature.

You will need
- White earthenware clay
- Black slip
- Paintbrushes
- Sgraffito tool
- Incising tool
- Transparent earthenware glaze

Arranging tiles
Definitely a feature, this tile works best in isolation within a plain scheme.

DESIGN IDEA

TECHNIQUE

DIFFICULTY

see also kilns and firing **18–21** drying tiles **37** transferring motifs **53**

MOTIF

Goose A goose motif always works wonderfully well in a country kitchen tile scheme, perhaps with other farmyard birds or animals.

CLAY Red earthenware fired to 2,012°F (1,100°C) biscuit and 1,976°F (1,080°C) glaze

Order of work

1 Prepare the tile and dry to leather hard.

2 Transfer the design onto the tile and sgraffito the outline.

3 After biscuit firing, fill in the sgraffito outline with black underglaze stain, then dip the tile in white tin glaze and carefully paint in the detail of the beak and feet with yellow underglaze stain.

4 Wax out the outline border and the goose then carefully sponge a thin cobalt carbonate solution over the exposed glaze using an open, natural sponge.

5 Fire to the appropriate glaze temperature.

You will need
- Red earthenware clay
- Sgraffito tool
- Underglaze stains
- White tin glaze
- Wax emulsion
- Cobalt carbonate
- Natural sponge

Arranging tiles
This particular tile looks great in a kitchen scheme of plain tiles and other similar images.

DESIGN IDEA

TECHNIQUE

DIFFICULTY

see also kilns and firing **18–21** drying tiles **37**

MOTIF

Chicken and Cockerel
These birds have a wonderfully free, painterly quality to them, which particularly suits their characters. You may need to practice a little to duplicate the image, but the effort will be well worth it.

MOTIF

CLAY Red earthenware fired to 2,012°F (1,100°C) biscuit and 1,976°F (1,080°C) glaze

Order of work

1 Prepare the tile and coat it with a base layer of white slip.

2 Allow the tile to dry, then transfer the image onto the surface.

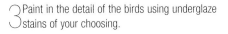

3 Paint in the detail of the birds using underglaze stains of your choosing.

4 After biscuit firing, cover with transparent glaze and fire to the required temperature.

You will need
• Red earthenware clay
• White slip
• Paintbrushes
• Selection of underglaze stains
• Transparent earthenware glaze

Arranging tiles
When randomly positioned in a plain tile scheme in a country kitchen, these tiles really come into their own.

TECHNIQUE

DIFFICULTY

see also kilns and firing **18–21** applying slip **32** drying tiles **37**

MOTIF

Stenciled Bird
This simple stencil can be used to brighten up a wall of plain tiles in any room of the house.

Order of work

1 Transfer the design to stencil card and carefully cut out the motif.

2 Position the stencil in place on a tile on the wall and use masking tape to secure it. Stipple in the detail using a selection of tile paints and a stencil brush.

3 Remove the stencil and seal the surface of the tile.

You will need
- Stencil card and a sharp craft knife
- Masking tape
- Selection of tile paints
- Stencil brush
- Surface sealant

Arranging tiles
The stencil can be used to repeat the design in numerous different colorways in a scheme of plain tiles.

DESIGN IDEA

TECHNIQUE

DIFFICULTY

see also kilns and firing **18–21** drying tiles **37** transferring motifs **53**

MOTIF

Birds in Flight

This motif is designed using a double repeat. This can be simply achieved by turning your tracing paper over to create a mirror image. Work on four tiles at a time so that you can properly see the repeat.

Order of work

1 Prepare four tiles and make two paper copies of the motif, one as a mirror image.

2 Apply a base coat of colored slip to the tiles.

3 Transfer the first copy of the motif onto two of the tiles and sgraffito in the detail.

4 Transfer the mirror-image motif onto the second two tiles and finish as before.

5 Apply a simple transparent glaze after biscuit firing, then fire to the appropriate temperature.

CLAY White earthenware fired to 2,012°F (1,100°C) biscuit and 1,976°F (1,080°C) glaze

You will need

- White earthenware clay
- Colored slip
- Sgraffito tool
- Transparent earthenware glaze
- Tracing paper

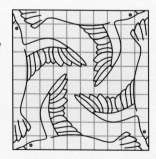

Arranging tiles

These tiles are designed to form a completely repeating scheme.

DESIGN IDEA

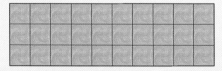

see also kilns and firing **18–21** drying tiles **37** transferring motifs **53**

TECHNIQUE

DIFFICULTY

MOTIF

Silver Fish
This shoal of fish would make a perfect feature swimming across the wall of a bathroom, and the image is easy to duplicate if you want to produce a batch of these tiles.

CLAY Red earthenware fired to 2,012°F (1,100°C) biscuit and 1,976°F (1,080°C) glaze. Luster firing to 1,346°F (730°C)

Order of work

1 Apply white tin glaze to a biscuit-fired tile.

2 Paint over the glaze with a thin wash of blue underglaze stain.

3 Transfer the motif to the tile and outline the fish with black underglaze stain using a very fine brush.

4 After glaze firing, paint or sponge in the bodies of the fish with silver luster and fire to the recommended temperature.

You will need
- Red earthenware clay
- White tin glaze
- Underglaze stains
- Very fine paintbrush
- Silver luster
- Natural sponge

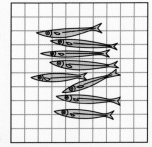

Arranging tiles
These tiles could be repeated in a scheme of similarly colored plain tiles.

DESIGN IDEA

TECHNIQUE

DIFFICULTY

1 **2**

see also kilns and firing **18–21** drying tiles **37** transferring motifs **53**

MOTIF

25

Leaping Fish This fish is inspired by a
William De Morgan design from the Arts and Crafts
period of the late 1900s.

CLAY Red earthenware fired to 2,012°F (1,100°C)
biscuit and 1,976°F (1,080°C) glaze

Order of work

1 Prepare the tile, coat with white slip, and dry to leather hard.

2 Transfer the design to the tile and sgraffito the outline.

3 After biscuit firing, apply a transparent colored glaze and fire to the appropriate temperature.

You will need

• Red earthenware clay
• White slip
• Paintbrushes
• Sgraffito tool
• Colored transparent earthenware glaze

Arranging tiles

This tile would work well positioned randomly in a scheme of plain tiles, or in columns as a frame or border.

DESIGN IDEAS

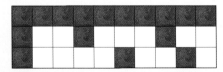

TECHNIQUE

DIFFICULTY

see also kilns and firing **18–21** drying tiles **37** transferring motifs **53**

MOTIF

26 Butterfly Fish
Tropical fish are fantastic subjects for depiction in ceramic because of the wealth of color and form they display, and the majolica technique used to paint this motif is perfect for the subject.

Order of work

1 Apply white tin glaze to a biscuit-fired tile and transfer the motif to the tile.

2 Using a selection of glaze or underglaze stains, paint in the detail of the fish and the coral behind it.

3 Carefully wax resist the outline of the fish and coral, then paint a thin wash of blue glaze or underglaze stain over the background to represent the water. Glaze fire the tile to the appropriate temperature.

CLAY Red earthenware fired to 2,012°F (1,100°C) biscuit and 1,976°F (1,080°C) glaze

You will need

• Red earthenware clay
• White tin glaze
• Paintbrushes
• Wax emulsion
• Selection of earthenware glaze or underglaze stains, including blue

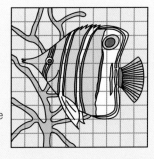

Arranging tiles

This tile would be best positioned randomly within a scheme of plain tiles with other similar designs interspersed.

DESIGN IDEA

TECHNIQUE		DIFFICULTY	

see also kilns and firing **18–21** drying tiles **37** wax resist **46** transferring motifs **53**

MOTIF

27

Jellyfish
A jellyfish is not strictly a fish, but it does live in water and makes a good motif for a tile, so for that reason it is included in this section.

CLAY Porcelain fired to 1,832°F (1,000°C) biscuit and 2,336°F (1,280°C) glaze

Order of work

1 Prepare the tile and monoprint the jellyfish motif onto it using cobalt oxide.

2 After biscuit firing the tile, apply a transparent glaze.

3 Fire to glaze temperature recommended.

You will need
- Porcelain clay
- Cobalt oxide
- Blue luster glaze
- Transparent porcelain glaze
- Paintbrushes or natural sponge

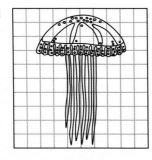

Arranging tiles
Arrange the tile as a feature in a plain scheme, with other similar images interspersed.

DESIGN IDEA

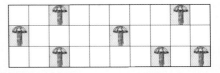

TECHNIQUE

DIFFICULTY

see also kilns and firing **18–21** drying tiles **37** transferring motifs **53**

MOTIF

28

Stenciled Fish
Fish stencils are relatively easy to cut and can add considerable interest to a wall of plain tiles in a bathroom or kitchen.

Order of work

1 Transfer the design to stencil card and carefully cut out the motif.

2 Position the stencil in place on the tile, using masking tape to secure it, and sponge in the detail using a selection of tile paints and a natural sponge.

3 Remove the stencil and seal the surface of the tile.

You will need
- Readymade tile
- Stencil card and a sharp craft knife
- Masking tape
- Selection of tile paints
- Natural sponge
- Surface sealant

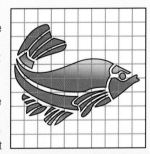

Arranging tiles
This stencil can be used to repeat the design in numerous different colorways within a scheme of plain tiles.

DESIGN IDEA

TECHNIQUE

DIFFICULTY

1

MOTIF

Clown Triggerfish

This is another colorful coral-reef fish with interesting markings and shape. It would look good with the majolica butterfly on page 98.

CLAY White earthenware fired to 2,012°F (1,100°C) biscuit and 1,868°F (1,020°C) glaze

Order of work

1 Carefully transfer the design to a dry but unfired tile.

2 Tube line the outline of the design.

3 After biscuit firing, paint in the detail of the fish using a selection of commercial paint-on glaze colors and fire to the recommended temperature.

You will need

- White earthenware clay
- Tube-lining slip
- Paintbrushes
- Selection of commercial paint-on glazes

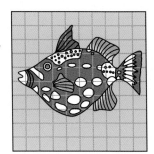

Arranging tiles

Mix randomly with other tiles of a similar style in a plain scheme.

DESIGN IDEA

TECHNIQUE

DIFFICULTY

see also kilns and firing **18–21** drying tiles **37** transferring motifs **53**

MOTIF

Angel Fish

Angel fish are visually both graceful and beautiful, and were a popular motif in the middle of the twentieth century for many art forms.

Order of work

1 Transfer the design to a leather-hard tile and carefully carve out the shape and the background.

2 After biscuit firing, coat the tile in white tin glaze and, when dry, wipe back the glaze so that it only remains in the carved-out detail.

3 Finely paint in color detail over the remaining glazed areas using underglaze stains, and fire to the appropriate temperature.

CLAY Red earthenware fired to 2,012°F (1,100°C) biscuit and 1,976°F (1,080°C) glaze

You will need
• Red earthenware clay
• Carving tools
• White earthenware tin glaze
• Paintbrushes
• Selection of underglaze stains

Arranging tiles
Mix randomly with other tiles of a similar style in a plain scheme.

DESIGN IDEA

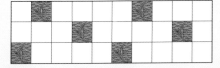

TECHNIQUE

DIFFICULTY

see also kilns and firing **18–21** drying tiles **37** transferring motifs **53**

MOTIF

31

Rustic Fish

This is perhaps one of the simplest motifs in the category, but it does require a sure hand to paint it freely, so it may help to practice on paper before committing to clay.

CLAY Red earthenware fired to 2,012°F (1,100°C) biscuit and 1,976°F (1,080°C) glaze

Order of work

1 Prepare the tile and apply a base coat of white slip.

2 When the tile has dried out completely, roughly paint over with a thin wash of underglaze stain.

3 Transfer the design to the tile and use black underglaze stain to paint in the detail as freely as possible. If you feel confident the motif could be painted freehand.

4 After biscuit firing, cover in transparent glaze and fire to the recommended temperature.

You will need

• Red earthenware clay
• White slip
• Paintbrushes
• Green and black underglaze stains
• Transparent earthenware glaze

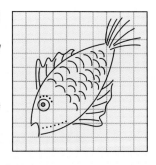

Arranging tiles

Mix randomly with other tiles of a similar style in a plain scheme.

DESIGN IDEA

TECHNIQUE

DIFFICULTY

1

see also kilns and firing **18–21** applying slip **32** drying tiles **37** underglaze painting **43** transferring motifs **53**

MOTIF

Pink Fish

This is another free, painterly style of motif with rustic appeal that demands a loose-handed application of color to make the fish look lively.

CLAY Red earthenware fired to 2,012°F (1,100°C) biscuit and 1,976°F (1,080°C) glaze

Order of work

1. Prepare the tile and apply a base coat of white slip.

2. When the tile has dried out, transfer the design to the surface.

3. Paint in the detail of the fish using underglaze stains, with a thin band of another color to frame it.

4. After biscuit firing, apply a transparent glaze and fire to the recommended temperature.

You will need
- Red earthenware clay
- White slip
- Paintbrushes
- Selection of underglaze stains
- Transparent earthenware glaze

Arranging tiles
Mix randomly with other tiles of a similar style in a plain scheme.

DESIGN IDEA

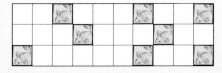

TECHNIQUE

DIFFICULTY

see also kilns and firing **18–21** applying slip **32** drying tiles **37** underglaze painting **43** transferring motifs **53**

MOTIF

Seahorse and Shells

The sprigs used to decorate this tile are mainly made from seashore finds, but the seahorse sprig was finely modeled in clay before casting in plaster. A simpler sprig could be modeled for similar effect.

CLAY Stoneware fired to 1,832°F (1,000°C) biscuit and 2,336°F (1,280°C) glaze

Order of work

1 Each maker's sprigs will be individual according to their own seashore finds, therefore the layout for the design is best decided by arranging the actual sprigs on a scale paper template of the tile.

2 Draw around the outline of each sprig to record the design. This will allow exact copies to be reproduced for future use.

3 Prepare the tile and transfer the layout to the surface of the clay and fix the sprigs in place.

4 After biscuit firing, apply an even coat of blue glaze, then wipe the glaze back over the sprigs using a damp cloth, leaving just a little in the texture of the sprigs to emphasize the fine detail.

You will need

- White stoneware clay
- Selection of sprigs made from seashore finds
- Blue stoneware glaze

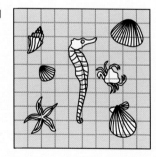

Arranging tiles

This tile looks good when randomly positioned as a feature in an expanse of plain tiles, in either the same glaze or a contrasting color, such as white.

DESIGN IDEA

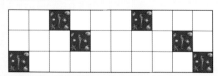

TECHNIQUE

DIFFICULTY

1

see also kilns and firing **18–21** making sprig molds **24–25** drying tiles **37** transferring motifs **53**

MOTIF

Majolica Butterfly This is a much
stylized butterfly, with a well-defined outline, making it
perfect for the majolica technique of decorating.

Order of work

1 Apply white tin glaze to a biscuit-fired tile.

2 Transfer the design to the tile and fill in the detail with a selection of underglaze stains.

3 Outline the butterfly with a thin line of black underglaze stain before glaze firing to the required temperature.

CLAY Red earthenware fired to 2,012°F (1,100°C) biscuit and 1,976°F (1,080°C) glaze

You will need

- Red earthenware clay
- White tin glaze
- Paintbrushes
- Selection of underglaze stains

Arranging tiles

This random motif could be loosely repeated in a scheme of plain tiles.

DESIGN IDEA

TECHNIQUE

DIFFICULTY

see also kilns and firing **18–21** drying tiles **37** transferring motifs **53**

MOTIF

Bumblebee Bees are such lovely insects
that they had to be included in this section, and paint-
on commercially prepared glazes are perfect for this motif
because they can be applied in a painterly way.

Insects

Order of work

1 Transfer the motif to a 6-in. (15-cm) square lino block and carefully cut out the detail using a fine cutting tool.

2 Prepare the tile and impress the lino block into it to transfer the design.

3 After biscuit firing, paint in the detail of the bee using a selection of commercial paint-on glazes, then fire to glaze temperature.

CLAY White earthenware fired to 2,012°F (1,100°C) biscuit and 1,868°F (1,020°C) glaze

You will need
- 6-in. (15-cm) square lino block
- Fine lino-cutting tool
- White earthenware clay
- Selection of commercial paint-on glazes

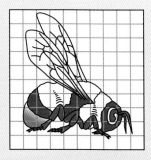

Arranging tiles
This tile would look great in an overall scheme with other insects and bugs.

DESIGN IDEA

TECHNIQUE

DIFFICULTY

see also kilns and firing **18–21** drying tiles **37** transferring motifs **53**

Simple Repeating Butterfly

This motif forms a simple repeat when the tiles are arranged so that the butterflies all point to the center, but they could equally well be positioned randomly for a different effect.

CLAY White stoneware fired to 1,832°F (1,000°C) biscuit and 2,300°F (1,260°C) glaze

Order of work

1 Apply a base color of glaze to a biscuit-fired tile.

2 Transfer the design to the tile, then wax out the outline using a fine brush.

3 Sponge over the motif using a selection of colored glazes, then fire to the appropriate temperature.

You will need

- White stoneware clay
- Selection of stoneware glazes
- Wax emulsion
- Fine paintbrush
- Natural sponge

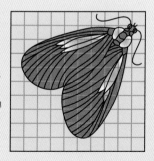

Arranging tiles

The best arrangement for these tiles is filling a wall in repeat.

DESIGN IDEA

TECHNIQUE

DIFFICULTY

see also kilns and firing **18–21** drying tiles **37** wax resist **46** transferring motifs **53**

Black-and-White Butterfly

Black-and-white butterflies make wonderfully graphic motifs for tiles that would look good anywhere in the house.

CLAY White stoneware fired to 1,832°F (1,000°C) biscuit and 2,300°F (1,260°C) glaze

Order of work

1 Prepare the tile and monoprint the butterfly motif onto it, ensuring that the clay is still soft.

2 After biscuit firing, apply a transparent glaze and fire to the recommended temperature.

You will need
- White stoneware clay
- Black body stain
- Transparent stoneware glaze
- Paintbrushes

Arranging tiles
A good place for this tile would be arranged among other butterflies in an overall scheme that includes some colored varieties.

DESIGN IDEA

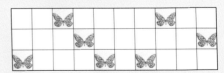

TECHNIQUE

DIFFICULTY

see also kilns and firing **18–21** drying tiles **37** transferring motifs **53**

MOTIF

38

Fly Many people may not like the idea of a fly as a motif, but they have remarkably interesting detail on their bodies, and some can be quite beautiful, despite their unsavory habits.

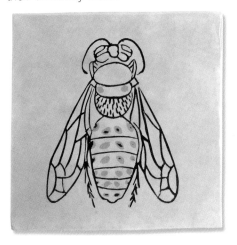

CLAY White earthenware fired to 2,012°F (1,100°C) biscuit and 1,976°F (1,080°C) glaze

Order of work

1 Prepare the tile and allow it to dry to leather hard.

2 Transfer the design to the tile and finely sgraffito the detail.

3 Infill the design with colored slips and, when the slip has dried sufficiently, scrape away the surplus to reveal the motif.

4 After biscuit firing, apply colored transparent glaze and fire to the required temperature.

You will need
- White earthenware clay
- Sgraffito tool
- Selection of colored slips
- Paintbrushes
- Colored transparent glaze

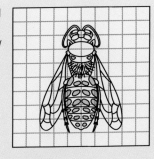

Arranging tiles
This tile is best positioned as a single feature in an expanse of plain tiles.

DESIGN IDEA

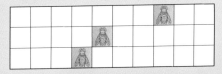

TECHNIQUE

DIFFICULTY

see also kilns and firing **18–21** drying tiles **37** transferring motifs **53**

MOTIF

39 Black-and-White Butterfly No. 2

This is another interpretation of a black-and-white butterfly, which could be displayed with the others in this chapter.

CLAY Porcelain fired to 1,832°F (1,000°C) biscuit and 2,336°F (1,280°C) glaze

Order of work

1 Prepare the tile and dry to leather hard.

2 Transfer the design to the tile and carefully incise it.

3 After biscuit firing, cover the motif with black glaze, then carefully wipe it back so that it only remains in the detail. Cover the area surrounding the butterfly with reactive glaze, then fire to glaze temperature.

You will need
- Porcelain clay
- Incising tool
- Black stoneware glaze
- Paintbrushes
- Reactive glaze

Arranging tiles
Try arranging this tile with others that have been made in the same way but glazed in different colors.

DESIGN IDEA

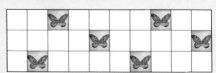

TECHNIQUE

DIFFICULTY

1 **2**

see also kilns and firing **18–21** drying tiles **37** wax resist **46** transferring motifs **53**

MOTIF

Butterfly-Wing Stencil

Some butterflies are so beautiful, but have too much detail to copy. A good solution is to look at one section of patterning only, which abstracts the image, creating something quite unique.

Order of work

1 Transfer the design to stencil card and carefully cut out the stencil.

2 Position the stencil in place on the tile, using masking tape to secure it, and sponge or stipple in the detail using a selection of tile paints.

3 Remove the stencil and seal the surface of the tile.

You will need
- Stencil card and a sharp craft knife
- Masking tape
- Selection of tile paints
- Natural sponge or stencil brush
- Surface sealant

Arranging tiles
This motif is a random design, but could be used to form a loose repeat if rotated so that the same angle of the design is central.

DESIGN IDEAS

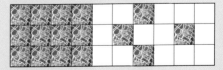

TECHNIQUE

DIFFICULTY

MOTIF

41 Dragonfly

Dragonflies are beautiful creatures, and the Raku technique of reduction firing is perfect to reflect the shimmering qualities of this insect, offset against a black background.

CLAY Grogged Raku clay fired to 1,832ºF (1,000ºC) biscuit and approximately 1,562ºF (850ºC) Raku glaze with a smoke reduction

Order of work

1 Make the sprig and fix it carefully onto a leather-hard tile.

2 After biscuit firing, wax out any areas of the tile that will be unglazed, then apply Raku glazes to the appropriate areas of the motif.

3 Raku fire the tile and reduce in sawdust to achieve the blackened background.

You will need
- Plaster
- Wax emulsion
- Raku clay
- Raku glazes
- Paintbrushes

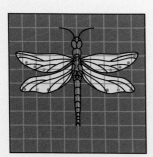

Arranging tiles
The tile would suit being randomly placed as a feature in a scheme of plain tiles.

DESIGN IDEA

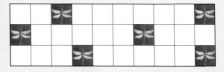

TECHNIQUE

DIFFICULTY

see also kilns and firing **18–21** raku firing **21** making sprig molds **24–25** drying tiles **37** wax resist **46** transferring motifs **53**

MOTIF

42

Stylized Butterfly Panel This

highly stylized butterfly panel is reminiscent of the designs of the 1960s, so to continue the psychedelic theme the panel is painted in bright glaze colors.

CLAY White earthenware fired to 2,012°F (1,100°C) biscuit and 1,976°F (1,080°C) glaze

Order of work

1 Transfer the design to a biscuit-fired tile then wax the outline using a fine brush.

2 Paint in the detail of the motif using a selection of commercial paint-on glazes and fire to the appropriate glaze temperature.

You will need
- White earthenware clay
- Wax emulsion
- Fine paintbrush
- Selection of commercial paint-on glazes
- Paintbrushes

Arranging tiles
These tiles form a good repeat that is well suited to column arrangements, as a frame or border.

DESIGN IDEA

TECHNIQUE

DIFFICULTY

see also kilns and firing **18–21** drying tiles **37** wax resist **46** transferring motifs **53**

MOTIF

43

Butterfly Ring
This simple butterfly motif would easily fit into any scheme in the home.

CLAY White stoneware fired to 1,832°F (1,000°C) biscuit and 2,336°F (1,280°C) glaze

Order of work

1 Prepare the tile and allow it to dry to leather hard.

2 Transfer the design to the tile and sgraffito it into the surface.

3 After biscuit firing, paint in the detail of the butterflies with a selection of underglaze colors, then apply a reactive or opalescent glaze and fire to the recommended temperature.

You will need
- White stoneware clay
- Sgraffito tool
- Transparent stoneware glaze
- Paintbrushes

Arranging tiles
The tile forms a simple repeat, so could be used to cover a whole area.

DESIGN IDEA

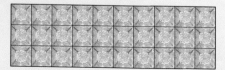

TECHNIQUE

DIFFICULTY

see also kilns and firing **18–21** drying tiles **37** underglaze painting **43** transferring motifs **53**

MOTIF

Octopus
This tile is modeled and cast in plaster for ease of mass production, but could be made by slip casting, as an alternative to the pressing method, if you prefer.

CLAY White stoneware fired to 1,832°F (1,000°C) biscuit and 2,336°F (1,280°C) glaze

Order of work

1 First model the tile and use the model to make a plaster mold.

2 Make the tile by rolling a slab of clay and pressing it into the plaster mold.

3 After biscuit firing, brush an oxide wash over the tile, then wipe it back with a damp sponge so that it remains in the detail only.

4 Apply a pale, colored transparent glaze and fire to the appropriate temperature.

You will need
• White stoneware clay
• Plaster
• Oxide
• Paintbrushes
• Pale, colored transparent stoneware glaze

Arranging tiles
The tile works equally well as a repeat or as a feature tile in a plain scheme.

DESIGN IDEAS

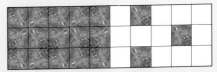

TECHNIQUE

DIFFICULTY

see also kilns and firing **18–21** mold making **22–23** drying tiles **37** oxide decoration **45–47** transferring motifs

45 Crab You will need a finely pointed tool to sgraffito the outline of this reasonably detailed crab into the clay.

Order of work

1 Prepare the tile and allow it to dry to leather hard.

2 Transfer the design to the surface of the tile and carefully sgraffito the outline of the crab and the frame.

3 Using a loop tool, or the end of the sgraffito tool, incise a pattern around the outer frame.

4 After biscuit firing, apply a colored glaze, then wipe it back so that it only remains in the detail of the tile. Fire to the recommended temperature.

CLAY White earthenware fired to 2,012ºF (1,100ºC) biscuit and 1,976ºF (1,080ºC) glaze

You will need

- White earthenware clay
- Sgraffito tool
- Loop tool (optional)
- Earthenware glaze
- Paintbrushes

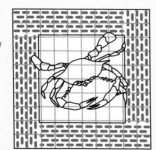

Arranging tiles

This tile would look especially effective as a feature in a scheme of plain tiles with other similar designs interspersed.

DESIGN IDEA

TECHNIQUE

DIFFICULTY

see also kilns and firing **18–21** drying tiles **37** transferring motifs **53**

MOTIF

Lobster This lobster motif is adapted from an American Arts and Crafts tile that was one of a series based on nursery rhymes and used to decorate primary schools.

CLAY Red or white earthenware fired to 2,012°F (1,100°C) biscuit and 1,868°F (1,020°C) glaze

Order of work

1 Prepare the tile and allow to dry to the leather-hard stage.

2 Transfer the design to the surface of the tile and carefully sgraffito the outline of the lobster and the frame.

3 After biscuit firing, paint in the detail of the lobster with a selection of commercial paint-on glaze colors before firing to the appropriate temperature.

You will need

- Red or white earthenware clay
- Sgraffito tool
- Selection of commercial paint-on glazes
- Paintbrushes

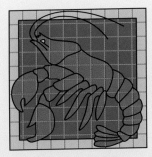

Arranging tiles

This tile would work well in a feature scheme with other tiles of the same style.

DESIGN IDEA

TECHNIQUE

DIFFICULTY

1

see also kilns and firing **18–21** drying tiles **37** transferring motifs **53**

Starfish On Sand
This tile could easily be used to fill a whole wall of a bathroom or wet room, because it requires a large expanse to best show off the repeat.

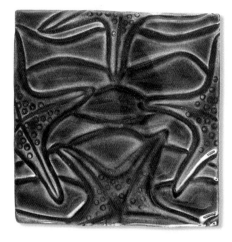

Order of work

1 Model the tile and use the model to make a plaster mold.

2 Make the tile by rolling a slab of clay and pressing it into the mold.

3 After the biscuit firing, apply a base glaze color with a second application of reactive glaze over the top, and fire to the recommended temperature.

CLAY White stoneware fired to 1,832°F (1,000°C) biscuit and 2,336°F (1,280°C) glaze

You will need
- White stoneware clay
- Plaster
- Stoneware glaze
- Paintbrushes
- Reactive glaze

Arranging tiles
These tiles form a complete repeat.

DESIGN IDEA

TECHNIQUE

DIFFICULTY

see also kilns and firing **18–21** mold making **22–23** drying tiles **37** transferring motifs **53**

MOTIF

Nautilus Shell
Nautilus shells have been popular subjects for artists all through history, presumably because of their wonderful shape and the patterning on the shell. For both of these reasons they lend themselves particularly well to stenciling.

Order of work

1 Transfer the motif to stencil card and carefully cut out the design.

2 Lay the stencil over a commercially glazed tile and secure in place with masking tape. Sponge a selection of enamel colors over the stencil and allow to dry.

3 Remove the stencil and seal the surface of the tile.

You will need
- Stencil card and a sharp craft knife
- Commercially glazed tile
- Masking tape
- Selection of enamel colors
- Natural sponge
- Sealant

Arranging tiles
These tiles would make an interesting border feature in a scheme of plain tiles.

DESIGN IDEA

TECHNIQUE

DIFFICULTY

see also kilns and firing **18–21** drying tiles **37** transferring motifs **53**

MOTIF

49

Shells

This is a simple tile to make and could be used to cover a whole wall if required. To do this, however, you could save time by casting the tile in plaster to make a mold for quick production.

CLAY White stoneware fired to 1,832°F (1,000°C) biscuit and 2,336°F (1,280°C) glaze

Order of work

1 Prepare the tile and allow it to dry to leather hard.

2 Transfer the design to the surface of the tile and carefully incise it.

3 After biscuit firing, apply a selection of underglaze stains to the shell details, then cover with an opalescent glaze and fire to glaze temperature.

You will need

- White stoneware clay
- Incising tools
- Stoneware glaze
- Opalescent glaze and underglaze stains

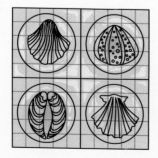

Arranging tiles

This design works very well as a repeat or as a feature in a scheme of plain tiles.

DESIGN IDEAS

TECHNIQUE

DIFFICULTY

1

see also kilns and firing **18–21** drying tiles **37** underglaze painting **43** transferring motifs **53**

MOTIF

Hydrozoan These microscopic inhabitants

of the sea are not visible to the naked eye, but are fantastic when viewed under a microscope, and make great motifs for tiles.

CLAY White stoneware fired to 1,832°F (1,000°C) biscuit and 2,336°F (1,280°C) glaze

Order of work

1 Apply a base coat of glaze to a biscuit-fired tile.

2 Transfer the motif to the surface of the tile, then wax out the outline detail.

3 Sponge over one or two more contrasting glaze colors before firing to temperature.

You will need

- White stoneware clay
- Selection of stoneware glazes
- Paintbrushes
- Wax emulsion
- Natural sponge

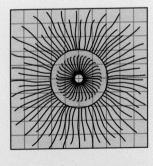

Arranging tiles

Mix with other tiles of a similar style randomly positioned within a plain scheme.

DESIGN IDEA

TECHNIQUE

DIFFICULTY

see also kilns and firing **18–21** drying tiles **37** wax resist **46** transferring motifs **53**

Coral
Amazingly, corals grow in a myriad of colors and patterns, which create endless inspiration for design.

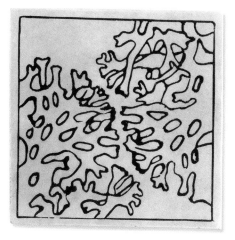

Order of work

1 Prepare the tile and allow to dry to the leather-hard stage.

2 Transfer the design to the tile surface and carefully sgraffito the outline of the coral, varying the thickness of the lines.

3 Fill the sgraffito outline with colored slip then, when leather hard, carefully scrape away the excess.

4 After biscuit firing, apply a colored transparent glaze and fire to the required temperature.

CLAY White earthenware fired to 2,012°F (1,100°C) biscuit and 1,976°F (1,080°C) glaze

You will need
- White earthenware clay
- Sgraffito tools
- Colored slip
- Paintbrushes
- Colored transparent earthenware glaze

Arranging tiles
This is a random tile to fit into a scheme of plain tiles.

DESIGN IDEA

TECHNIQUE

DIFFICULTY

 1 2

see also kilns and firing **18–21** drying tiles **37** transferring motifs **53**

MOTIF

52

Yacht
This motif is ideally suited to the majolica style of decoration, which gives a painterly, atmospheric quality to the image.

CLAY Red earthenware fired to 2,012°F (1,100°C) biscuit and 1,976°F (1,080°C) glaze

Order of work

1. Apply a covering of white tin glaze to a biscuit-fired tile.

2. Transfer the motif to the surface of the tile.

3. Using a selection of underglaze stains, paint in the detail of the motif, then fire to the required temperature.

You will need
- Red earthenware clay
- White tin glaze
- Paintbrushes
- Selection of underglaze stains

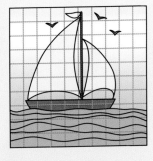

Arranging tiles
This tile looks good when randomly positioned as a feature in an expanse of plain tiles, with other similar motifs interspersed.

DESIGN IDEA

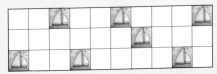

TECHNIQUE

DIFFICULTY

see also kilns and firing **18–21** drying tiles **37** transferring motifs **53**

MOTIF

Stenciled Shells

Shells can be found in many interesting shapes and sizes, and their patterning lends them particularly well to stencil decoration, which can be used to brighten up a dull wall of tiles for very little cost.

Order of work

1 Transfer the motif to stencil card and carefully cut out the design.

2 Lay the stencil over the tile on the wall and secure with masking tape. Stipple or sponge a selection of tile paints over the stencil before carefully removing it.

3 Move the stencil to the next tile to continue the sequence. For added interest you could turn the stencil around so that the shells are at a different angle.

4 Seal the surface of the tile.

You will need

- Stencil card and a sharp craft knife
- Masking tape
- Selection of tile paints
- Stencil brush or natural sponge
- Surface sealant

Arranging tiles

The stencil could be used either as a random repeat mixed with plain tiles, or to create a border or frame.

DESIGN IDEAS

TECHNIQUE

DIFFICULTY

 1

MOTIF

MOTIF

Fossilized Coral This can be especially beautiful and patternlike, and this tile draws upon these qualities to create a simple but effective motif.

Order of work

1 Mix together iron oxide and transparent earthenware glaze to form a paste about the consistency of light cream.

2 Paint an even coat of the oxide mixture over a ready-glazed commercial tile and allow it to dry thoroughly.

3 Trace the design onto a tile-sized sheet of paper, then place the paper tracing over the tile and redraw the outline.

4 Carefully lift the paper away from the tile. The paper should have lifted the oxide from the surface where it was drawn. Neaten up the drawing on the tile with a pointed tool if necessary, then fire the tile to 1,976°F (1,080°C).

You will need

- Iron oxide
- Transparent earthenware glaze
- Ready-glazed commercial tile
- Paintbrushes
- Paper and pencil

Arranging tiles

This tile would look good as a random feature in a scheme of pale blue tiles.

DESIGN IDEA

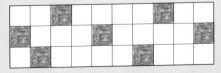

TECHNIQUE

DIFFICULTY

see also kilns and firing **18–21** drying tiles **37** oxide decoration **45–47** transferring motifs **53**

MOTIF

55 Fern

The ferns growing today are hardly changed from their fossil predecessors, and make wonderful impressions in clay. Ferns grow almost anywhere, so you should easily be able to find a sample.

CLAY Red earthenware fired to 2,012°F (1,100°C) biscuit and 1,976°F (1,080°C) glaze

Order of work

1 Roll a fern leaf onto a soft slab of clay.

2 Dampen the surface of a plaster bat (the back of one of your tile molds will do) and paint a rough layer of colored slip over it.

3 Turn the slab of clay, with the fern still on the surface, over onto the slipped bat and roll gently.

4 Lift the slab off the bat. Not all of the slip will lift from the bat, giving the clay slab a rocklike look. Cut the tile to size and remove the fern.

5 After biscuit firing, paint a manganese dioxide wash over the fern motif on the tile, then wipe back. Cover with transparent glaze and fire to the recommended temperature.

You will need

- Red earthenware clay
- Fern leaves
- Plaster bat
- Colored slip
- Paintbrushes
- Manganese dioxide
- Transparent earthenware glaze

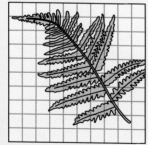

Arranging tiles

This tile could be used either randomly or in repeat. To make the tile repeat exactly, make a plaster mold of the biscuit-fired tile.

DESIGN IDEAS

TECHNIQUE

DIFFICULTY

see also kilns and firing **18–21** drying tiles **37** oxide decoration **45–47** transferring motifs **53**

MOTIF

56 Fossil Fish

Cutting the outline of this fossil fish from a lino block is a little tricky, but ever so realistic when the tile is made.

CLAY Buff grogged stoneware fired to 1,832°F (1,000°C) biscuit and 2,300°F (1,260°C) glaze

Order of work

1 Transfer the design to a lino block and cut out the outline.

2 Paint a rough coat of earthy colored slip over the surface of a slab of clay, and dry off to the touch.

3 Roll the lino block over the slab. Lift the lino block off the slab and cut the tile to size.

4 After biscuit firing, apply transparent glaze and fire to glaze temperature.

You will need
- 6-in. (15-cm) square lino block
- Buff grogged stoneware clay
- Colored slip
- Paintbrushes
- Transparent stoneware glaze

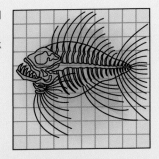

Arranging tiles
This tile would look especially effective in an exterior location, such as within a garden wall or path.

DESIGN IDEA

TECHNIQUE

DIFFICULTY

1 **2** 3

see also kilns and firing **18–21** applying slip **32** drying tiles **37** transferring motifs **53**

Shells and Ammonites

The shapes of shells have changed little through the ages, so use your beach finds. If you do not have access to shells or ammonites, stamp models can be made in clay and fired for endless use.

CLAY White earthenware fired to 2,012°F (1,100°C) biscuit and 1,976°F (1,080°C) glaze

Order of work

1 Make a selection of shell and ammonite stamps from clay and biscuit fire them.

2 Make a rocklike slab of clay by ripping a slab and roughly rejoining it, so that when rolled out again the edges are clearly visible. Cut a tile from the slab.

3 Roughly paint over the tile with two or three slip colors, then use the stamps to make the impressions.

4 After biscuit firing, paint manganese dioxide in the fossil textures and wipe back a little. Apply transparent glaze and fire to the required temperature.

You will need

- White earthenware clay
- Selection of colored slips
- Paintbrushes
- Manganese dioxide
- Transparent earthenware glaze

Arranging tiles

This tile could be used as a random feature in a scheme of plain tiles, or as a repeat to cover a bathroom wall.

DESIGN IDEA

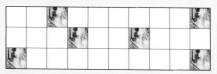

TECHNIQUE

DIFFICULTY

1 2

see also kilns and firing **18–21** applying slip **32** drying tiles **37** oxide decoration **45–47** transferring motifs **53**

MOTIF

58

Ammonite Group

Sprig molds for this tile can be made by casting samples of real ammonite fossils in plaster, by carving the detail into a clay model and casting this, or by carving the ammonite from a small block of plaster.

CLAY Raku clay fired to 1,832°F (1,000°C) biscuit and approximately 1,652°F (900°C) Raku glaze with a smoke reduction

Order of work

1 Make a sprig mold using one of the techniques described above.

2 Fix the sprigs onto the surface of a leather-hard tile, using a toothbrush and water to score the undersides and the corresponding position on the tile.

3 Make sure no air is trapped under the sprigs before leaving to dry out.

4 After biscuit firing, apply turquoise Raku glaze to the surface of the tile, then wipe it back a little so as not to lose the definition of markings in the ammonites. Raku fire and reduce in sawdust before cleaning off the tile with water and a scouring pad.

You will need

- Raku clay
- Potter's plaster
- Toothbrush
- Turquoise Raku glaze
- Paintbrush
- Scouring pad

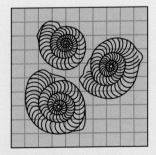

Arranging tiles

These tiles could be used randomly in a scheme of tiles of a similar color, or in repeat for a feature wall.

DESIGN IDEAS

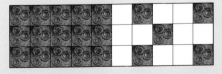

TECHNIQUE

DIFFICULTY

see also kilns and firing **18–21** raku firing **21** making sprig molds **24–25** drying tiles **37**

Starfish Fossil
This starfish was carved out of a tile-sized block of plaster. This is a quick and easy way of creating a relief surface, because the clay can then be rolled directly over the plaster.

CLAY Red earthenware fired to 2,012°F (1,100°C) biscuit only

Order of work

1 Make a few plain, tile-sized plaster blocks about 1 ¼ in. (3 cm) thick—you only need one, but it is handy to have some extras ready for future use.

2 Transfer the motif to the surface of the plaster block, then carve out the detail with a sharp modeling tool.

3 Roll out a slab of clay then place it over the plaster carving and roll to the correct thickness.

4 Lift the clay off the plaster and cut the tile to size. Paint over the tile with a thin wash of white slip and wipe back gently over the fossil.

5 Paint a thin wash of copper oxide over the tile and wipe away any excess, before firing to biscuit temperature.

You will need
- Potter's plaster
- Modeling tool
- Red earthenware clay
- Rolling pin and roller guides
- White slip
- Paintbrushes
- Copper oxide

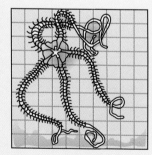

Arranging tiles
This tile could be used randomly in a scheme of tiles made in the same way but with different fossil motifs, or in repeat with the tile turned so that the fossil lies in different positions.

DESIGN IDEAS

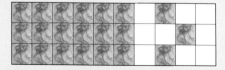

TECHNIQUE

DIFFICULTY

see also kilns and firing **18–21** mold making **22–23** applying slip **32** drying tiles **37** oxide decoration **45–47** transferring motifs **53**

MOTIF

Large Ammonite

This large ammonite is carved into a thicker-than-average tile, and fired to stoneware temperature, making it ideal for an outdoor location on a wall or pathway.

CLAY Buff colored grogged stoneware fired to 1,832°F (1,000°C) biscuit and 2,336°F (1,280°C) for vitrification

Order of work

1 Roll out a tile to about 6 in. (15 cm) thick, and allow to dry to the leather-hard stage.

2 Transfer the design to the surface of the tile, then carve out the detail so that the ammonite has a more three-dimensional appearance.

3 After biscuit firing, paint over the ammonite with a thick wash of copper oxide, then fire to 2,336°F (1,280°C) to vitrify the clay.

You will need
- Buff colored grogged stoneware clay (such as crank)
- Modeling tool
- Copper oxide
- Paintbrush

Arranging tiles
This tile could be used either randomly or in repeat in an exterior setting.

DESIGN IDEA

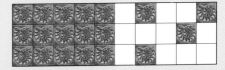

TECHNIQUE

DIFFICULTY

see also kilns and firing **18–21** drying tiles **37** oxide decoration **45–47** transferring motifs **53**

MOTIF

Sea Urchin This is a simple tile to make, but requires a little patience to pierce all the holes. You will need a selection of pointed tools to produce a variety of marks.

Fossils

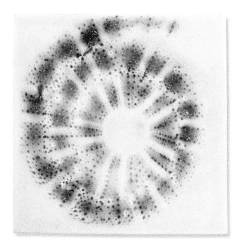

CLAY Porcelain fired to 1,832°F (1,000°C) biscuit and 2,300°F (1,260°C) glaze

Order of work

1 Prepare the tile and allow it to dry to leather hard.

2 Transfer the design to the surface of the tile, then use a selection of pointed tools—to vary the quality of mark—to impress the dotty areas of the motif into the clay.

3 After biscuit firing, paint over the tile with a wash of copper carbonate, then wipe it back slightly.

4 Cover with transparent glaze and fire to glaze temperature.

You will need
- Porcelain clay
- Selection of pointed tools
- Copper carbonate
- Paintbrush
- Transparent stoneware glaze

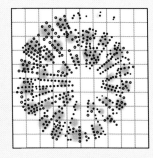

Arranging tiles
This tile would look very good randomly positioned in a plain scheme of tiles of a similar colorway.

DESIGN IDEA

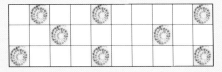

TECHNIQUE

DIFFICULTY

see also kilns and firing **18–21** drying tiles **37** oxide decoration **45–47** transferring motifs **53**

125

MOTIF

Aquilegia Vulgaris
Seedheads from the actual plant have been used to make this simple tile, but the motif can easily be incised to create a similar finish. Alternatively, use whatever seedheads you can find.

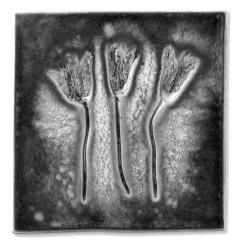

CLAY Porcelain fired to 1,832°F (1,000°C) biscuit and 2,336°F (1,280°C) glaze

Order of work

1 Roll the seedheads into a slab of porcelain clay in a simple line, then cut the tile to size so that the seedheads are central.

2 After biscuit firing, apply a thin wash of oxide to the seedhead impressions.

3 Finish by applying a transparent or opaque glaze and fire to the recommended temperature.

You will need
- Seedheads
- Porcelain clay
- Rolling pin
- Oxide
- Paintbrushes
- Transparent stoneware glaze

Arranging tiles
Randomly position these tiles with others in the same style to fill a whole scheme.

DESIGN IDEA

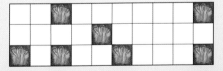

TECHNIQUE

DIFFICULTY

 1

see also kilns and firing **18–21** drying tiles **37** oxide decoration **45–47** transferring motifs **53**

Tulip Pattern

This motif is a simple sponged repeat in the majolica style with wax resist, so that there is a contrast between the clay and the glaze.

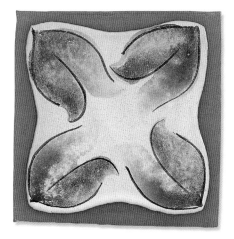

CLAY Red earthenware fired to 2,012°F (1,100°C) biscuit and 1,976°F (1,080°C) glaze

Order of work

1 Transfer the design to the surface of a biscuit-fired tile and wax out the border edge.

2 Apply white tin glaze to the center of the tile.

3 Cut a sponge to the shape of the motif.

4 Use the cut sponge to apply two or three colors of underglaze stain to the surface of the tile in the pattern shown, then fire to the required glaze temperature.

You will need

- Red earthenware clay
- Wax emulsion
- Paintbrushes
- White tin glaze
- Synthetic sponge
- Craft knife
- Selection of underglaze stains

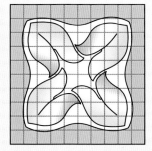

Arranging tiles

These tiles could work either randomly positioned in a scheme of plain terracotta tiles, or as a border repeat.

DESIGN IDEAS

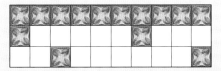

TECHNIQUE

DIFFICULTY

see also kilns and firing **18–21** drying tiles **37** wax resist **46** transferring motifs **53**

Stylized Leaf Design

This tile requires a little lateral thinking to get the sequence of paper resist application right, so the relative sections have been numbered to make it less testing.

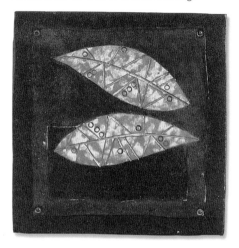

CLAY White earthenware fired to 2,012°F (1,100°C) biscuit and 1,976°F (1,080°C) glaze

Order of work

1 Cut out the paper sections from newspaper and number them accordingly.

2 Apply a base coat of slip color to a leather-hard tile.

3 Dampen and apply the paper sections numbered 1 and 3, then apply a second slip color.

4 Remove the paper sections then dampen and apply the negative of the cutout leaves, 2, and sponge over one or two more slip colors.

5 Sgraffito the fine detail.

6 Apply a transparent glaze after biscuit firing, then fire to the recommended temperature.

You will need

- Newspaper
- White earthenware clay
- Selection of colored slips
- Paintbrushes
- Natural sponge
- Sgraffito tool
- Transparent earthenware glaze

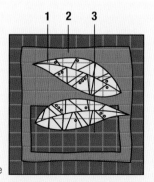

Arranging tiles

A good situation for this tile is as a randomly repeated feature in a scheme of plain tiles.

DESIGN IDEA

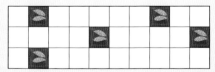

TECHNIQUE

DIFFICULTY

see also kilns and firing **18–21** applying slip **32** drying tiles **37** transferring motifs **53**

Allium Seedhead
Alliums are fantastic garden flowers, but the seedheads are equally fantastic, and make a great motif that looks especially contemporary.

Order of work

1 Prepare the tile and allow to dry to the leather-hard stage.

2 Transfer the design to the clay and finely sgraffito the outline of the seedhead.

3 Infill the design with white slip and, when the slip has dried sufficiently, scrape away the surplus to reveal the motif.

4 This low-firing clay needs only to be biscuit fired.

CLAY Black earthenware fired to 1,832°F (1,000°C) biscuit only

You will need
- Black earthenware clay
- Sgraffito tool
- White slip
- Paintbrushes

Arranging tiles
This tile would look great with other seedhead tiles made in the same way.

DESIGN IDEA

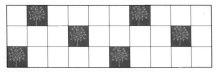

TECHNIQUE

DIFFICULTY

see also kilns and firing **18–21** drying tiles **37** transferring motifs **53**

MOTIF

Potted Tree

You will need a selection of different sized cutting tools for the lino block used to print this tile, and it is slightly difficult to cut, so you may want to practice a little first on lino scraps.

CLAY White stoneware fired to 1,832°F (1,000°C) biscuit and 2,300°F (1,260°C) glaze

Order of work

1 Transfer the design to a lino block and carefully cut it out using a range of cutting tools.

2 Prepare the tile and impress the lino block into it to transfer the design.

3 After biscuit firing, apply a wash of copper carbonate then cover with reactive or opalescent glaze and fire to glaze temperature.

You will need
- 6-in. (15-cm) square lino block
- Lino tools
- White stoneware clay and glaze
- Paintbrushes
- Copper carbonate

Arranging tiles
This style of tile would work very well as a frame or border, around a fireplace perhaps.

DESIGN IDEA

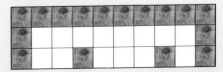

TECHNIQUE

DIFFICULTY

see also kilns and firing **18–21** drying tiles **37** oxide decoration **45–47** transferring motifs **53**

67 Old English Tile This motif is adapted from an old English encaustic style, and is made to look more rustic by the application of a honey glaze, which warms up the appearance of the clay and slip.

CLAY Red earthenware fired to 2,012°F (1,100°C) biscuit and 1,976°F (1,080°C) glaze

Order of work

1 Prepare the tile and dry to leather hard.

2 Transfer the design to the surface of the tile and sgraffito the outline detail.

3 Fill in the sgraffito lines with white slip, then, when the slip is dry enough, scrape it back to reveal the motif.

4 After biscuit firing, cover the tile with honey glaze and fire to the appropriate temperature.

You will need

- Red earthenware clay
- Sgraffito tool
- White slip
- Paintbrushes
- Honey transparent earthenware glaze

Arranging tiles

These tiles form a good enough repeat to fill the whole wall of a country kitchen.

DESIGN IDEA

see also kilns and firing **18–21** drying tiles **37** transferring motifs **53**

MOTIF

Leaf Vine
This tile is designed to repeat in columns, so would look especially effective on either side of a fireplace or doorway, as a special feature.

CLAY White stoneware fired to 1,832°F (1,000°C) biscuit and 2,300°F (1,260°C) glaze

Order of work

1 Prepare the tile and allow it to dry to leather hard.

2 Transfer the design to the surface of the tile and carve out the detail.

3 Make a plaster mold of the tile.

4 Make the tile by rolling a slab of clay and pressing it into the plaster mold.

5 After biscuit firing, apply an oxide wash and a glaze, then fire to the recommended temperature.

You will need
- White stoneware clay
- Carving tools
- Plaster
- Oxide
- Paintbrushes
- Stoneware glaze

Arranging tiles
Arrange the tiles in columns as a frame for doorways or fireplaces.

DESIGN IDEA

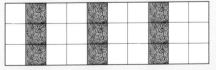

TECHNIQUE

DIFFICULTY

see also kilns and firing **18–21** mold making **22–23** drying tiles **37** oxide decoration **45–47** transferring motifs **53**

Woodland Floor

The arrangement of leaves in this design is meant to suggest a layout for the positioning of actual leaves on the clay, but you could sgraffito the design instead, if you do not have access to the real things.

CLAY White stoneware fired to 1,832°F (1,000°C) biscuit and 2,300°F (1,260°C) glaze

Order of work

1 Place a selection of differently shaped leaves over a slab of clay and roll them into the surface.

2 Select a good area and cut out the tile using a tile template.

3 After biscuit firing, apply an oxide wash to the surface of the tile, then cover with glaze and fire to the required temperature.

You will need

- White stoneware clay
- Selection of leaves
- Rolling pin
- Oxide
- Paintbrushes
- Stoneware glaze

Arranging tiles

This tile looks great as a random feature in a scheme of plain tiles.

DESIGN IDEA

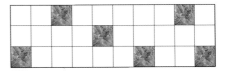

TECHNIQUE

DIFFICULTY

 1

see also kilns and firing **18–21** drying tiles **37** oxide decoration **45–47** transferring motifs **53**

MOTIF

70 Foliage

This Arts and Crafts-style tile has a tube-lined look, but is actually made from a linocut. It looks best covered with a simple glaze that will break over the detail.

CLAY White earthenware fired to 2,012°F (1,100°C) biscuit and 1,976°F (1,080°C) glaze

Order of work

1 Transfer the design to a lino block and carefully cut it out using a range of cutting tools.

2 Prepare the tile and impress the lino block into it to transfer the design.

3 After biscuit firing, apply a transparent colored glaze and fire to the required temperature.

You will need

- 6-in. (15-cm) square lino block
- Lino-cutting tools
- White earthenware clay
- Transparent colored glaze
- Paintbrushes

Arranging tiles

This tile forms a repeat if each tile is rotated so that the same corners meet in the middle, but it also looks equally good in columns for a frame or as a border.

DESIGN IDEA

TECHNIQUE

DIFFICULTY

1 **2**

see also kilns and firing **18–21** drying tiles **37** transferring motifs **53**

Wallpaper Texture Flower This is

a really simple tile to make, and one that can easily be varied by using different wallpaper textures.

CLAY White stoneware fired to 2,012°F (1,100°C) biscuit and 2,300°F (1,260°C) glaze

Order of work

1 Transfer the design to some textured wallpaper and cut out the petals and center.

2 Position the paper sections on a prepared tile, textured side down, and roll them into place using roller guides, then carefully remove them. Cut the outline of the tile back to shape.

3 After biscuit firing, apply an underglaze stain wash over the texture, then cover with opalescent glaze and fire to the recommended temperature.

You will need

- Textured wallpaper
- White stoneware clay
- Rolling pin, guides and knife
- Stoneware glaze
- Underglaze stains

Arranging tiles

These tiles would look really good on a wall in lots of different colorways, or as a repeat glazed all in white.

DESIGN IDEA

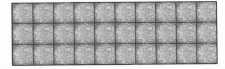

TECHNIQUE

DIFFICULTY

see also kilns and firing **18–21** drying tiles **37** underglaze painting **43** transferring motifs **53**

MOTIF

72

Single Impressed Leaf
If possible, find a leaf with a good vein structure for this tile, or copy the motif shown and sgraffito in the fine detail.

CLAY Porcelain fired to 1,832°F (1,000°C) biscuit and 2,336°F (1,280°C) glaze

Order of work

1 Prepare the tile and roll a leaf into the center, with the veined side down on the clay.

2 After biscuit firing, paint a thin oxide wash over the leaf.

3 Finish with a coat of transparent glaze and fire to the appropriate temperature.

You will need
- Porcelain clay
- A veined leaf
- Rolling pin
- Oxide
- Paintbrushes
- Transparent stoneware glaze

Arranging tiles
A good arrangement for this tile is randomly positioned with others of the same style in a scheme of plain tiles.

DESIGN IDEA

TECHNIQUE

DIFFICULTY
1

see also kilns and firing **18–21** drying tiles **37** underglaze painting **43** oxide decoration **45–47** transferring motifs **53**

Tube-Lined Tulip The outline of this

tulip is raised, so that when it is glazed the color will break over the surface to keep the flower shape well defined.

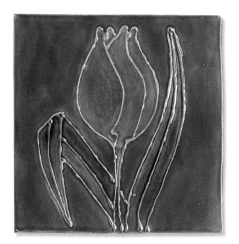

CLAY White earthenware fired to 2,012°F (1,100°C) biscuit and 1,868°F (1,020°C) glaze

Order of work

1 Carefully transfer the design to a dry but unglazed tile.

2 Tube line the outline of the design.

3 After biscuit firing, fill in the details of the motif with a selection of commercial paint-on glazes and fire to glaze temperature.

You will need

- White earthenware clay
- Tube-lining slip
- Paintbrushes
- Selection of commercial paint-on glazes

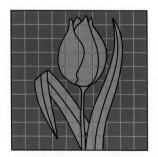

Arranging tiles

A feature tile like this one will fit into a scheme of plain tiles mixed with others in a similar style, but using different motifs.

DESIGN IDEA

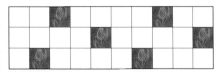

TECHNIQUE

DIFFICULTY

see also kilns and firing **18–21** drying tiles **37** underglaze painting **43** transferring motifs **53**

MOTIF

74

Sponged Leaf Design

This tile is made using a sponge leaf shape, wax resist, and stoneware glazes that react with one another to create interesting effects.

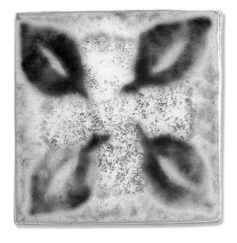

CLAY White stoneware fired to 1,832°F (1,000°C) biscuit and 2,300°F (1,260°C) glaze

Order of work

1 Apply a base glaze color to the surface of a biscuit-fired tile.

2 Transfer the design to the surface of the tile and wax out the borders around the leaf shapes.

3 Cut a sponge to the shape of a leaf motif.

4 Use the cut sponge to apply a second glaze color to the surface of the tile.

5 Wax over the leaf motif, then loosely sponge a final glaze color over the whole tile and fire to the recommended temperature.

You will need
- White stoneware clay
- Three stoneware glazes
- Wax emulsion
- Synthetic sponge
- Craft knife
- Natural sponge

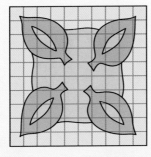

Arranging tiles

This tile would make a good repeat for a frame or border.

DESIGN IDEA

TECHNIQUE

DIFFICULTY

1 **2**

see also kilns and firing **18–21** drying tiles **37** underglaze painting **43** wax resist **46** transferring motifs **53**

Grasses and Leaves
These delicate grasses and leaves are the perfect subject material for the inlay technique of decoration, because of their simplicity.

Order of work

1 Prepare the tile and allow to dry to the leather-hard stage.

2 Transfer the design to the tile then sgraffito in the outline.

3 Infill the design with colored slips and, when the slip has dried sufficiently, scrape away the surplus to reveal the motif.

4 After biscuit firing, apply a transparent glaze and fire to the required temperature.

CLAY White earthenware fired to 2,012°F (1,100°C) biscuit and 1,976°F (1,080°C) glaze

You will need
- White earthenware clay
- Sgraffito tool
- Selection of colored slips
- Paintbrushes
- Transparent earthenware glaze

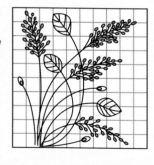

Arranging tiles
These tiles are meant as a random motif, but could actually form a repeat if rotated so that the center point is always the same.

DESIGN IDEA

TECHNIQUE

DIFFICULTY

see also kilns and firing **18–21** drying tiles **37** underglaze painting **43** transferring motifs **53**

MOTIF

Honeysuckle This is another motif in the Arts and Crafts style, which looks as good in a modern interior as in a country home.

Order of work

1 Prepare the tile and allow it to dry to leather hard.

2 Transfer the design to the surface of the tile and carefully scraffito it.

3 Inlay the sgraffito lines with colored slip, then scrape back when dry enough to reveal the lines.

4 Apply a colored transparent glaze and fire to the glaze temperature.

CLAY White stoneware fired to 2,012ºF (1,100ºC) biscuit and 1,976ºF (1,080ºC) glaze

You will need

- White earthenware clay
- Incising tools
- Earthenware glaze
- Paintbrushes
- Colored slip

Arranging tiles

This motif is designed to form a complete repeat.

DESIGN IDEA

Umbellifer
This is a general name for many of the country flowers seen along the roadside, which some may consider to be weeds. However, the flowers are actually very beautiful and make great motifs.

Order of work

1 Apply white tin glaze to a biscuit-fired tile, then paint a rough wash of underglaze stain in the approximate area of the flower head.

2 Transfer the design to the surface of the tile.

3 Paint in the fine detail of the flower using black underglaze stain, then fire to the appropriate glaze temperature.

CLAY Red earthenware fired to 2,012°F (1,100°C) biscuit and 1,976°F (1,080°C) glaze

You will need
- Red earthenware clay
- White tin glaze
- Paintbrushes
- Selection of underglaze stains, including black

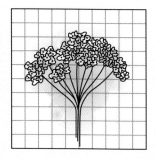

Arranging tiles
Mix this random design in a scheme of plain tiles with other motifs of the same style.

DESIGN IDEA

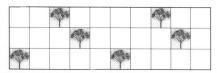

see also kilns and firing **18–21** drying tiles **37** underglaze painting **43** transferring motifs **53**

TECHNIQUE

DIFFICULTY

MOTIF

Stenciled Peony

This stencil would liven up any wall of plain tiles, but would fit especially well into a luxurious bathroom, with the aged gold detail giving it an opulent quality.

Order of work

1 Transfer the design to stencil card and carefully cut out the motif.

2 Use masking tape to fix the stencil in place over the tile and sponge over a layer of black tile paint.

3 When the paint has dried, lift the stencil and reposition it slightly off-register, then roughly paint over it with gold tile paint, leaving some areas exposed to look worn or aged.

4 Seal the surface of the tile.

You will need

- Stencil card and a sharp craft knife
- Masking tape
- Black and gold tile paint
- Natural sponge
- Surface sealant

Arranging tiles

This is a random motif, but it could be used to create a border repeat.

DESIGN IDEA

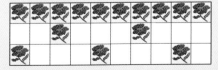

TECHNIQUE

DIFFICULTY

MOTIF

Sponged Flower This tile motif is
created from a precut sponge and on-glaze enamels.
You can use commercially glazed tiles instead of your own for this
motif, which cuts down on time considerably.

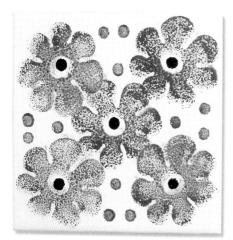

Order of work

1 Cut a sponge to the shape of the motif.

2 Mix some on-glaze enamel colors to the required consistency.

3 Use the cut sponge and the first enamel color to stamp the flowers, then fill in the details with another color or two.

4 Fire to 1,440°F (780°C).

You will need
- Synthetic sponge
- Craft knife
- Selection of on-glaze enamel colors
- Commercially glazed tile

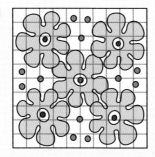

Arranging tiles
These tiles form a simple, complete repeat.

DESIGN IDEA

TECHNIQUE

DIFFICULTY

see also kilns and firing **18–21** applying underglaze colors with shaped sponges **43**

MOTIF

Half-Sized Tiles: Papaver

These half-sized tiles can be fitted into a scheme of full-sized tiles if properly positioned. The motifs are based on botanical studies.

Order of work

1 Prepare the tiles and apply a base coat of colored slip to the surface.

2 Transfer the design to the surface, then sgraffito the detail.

3 After biscuit firing, apply a transparent glaze and fire to the recommended glaze temperature.

CLAY White earthenware fired to 1,832°F (1,000°C) biscuit and 2,300°F (1,260°C) glaze

You will need
- White earthenware clay
- Incising tools
- Sgraffito tool
- Selection of colored slips
- Paintbrushes

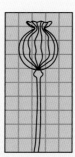

Arranging tiles
These tiles are designed to fit randomly into a scheme of plain tiles.

DESIGN IDEA

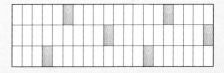

TECHNIQUE

DIFFICULTY

see also kilns and firing **18–21** applying slip **32** drying tiles **37** transferring motifs **53**

MOTIF

 Lilium Martagom

MOTIF

 Iris Pseudacorus

MOTIF

 Isatis Tinctoria

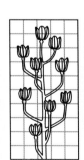

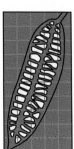

MOTIF

Carrots
This is a very simple tile to make, and requires the minimum of tools and materials, yet it looks very effective. Try making other vegetables in the same style.

CLAY Red earthenware fired to 2,012°F (1,100°C) biscuit and 1,976°F (1,080°C) glaze

Order of work

1 Prepare the tile and allow it to dry to leather hard.

2 Transfer the design to the tile and carefully sgraffito the outline.

3 After biscuit firing, brush over the tile with a thin black iron oxide wash, then wax out the area immediately around the carrots.

4 Apply a honey transparent glaze to the tile and fire to the recommended temperature.

You will need
- Red earthenware clay
- Sgraffito tool
- Black iron oxide
- Paintbrushes
- Wax emulsion
- Honey earthenware glaze

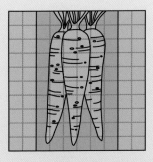

Arranging tiles
Fit the tile randomly into a scheme with plain tiles and other motifs in the same style.

DESIGN IDEA

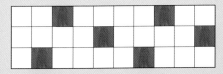

TECHNIQUE

DIFFICULTY

1

see also kilns and firing **18–21** drying tiles **37** oxide decoration **45–47** transferring motifs **53**

MOTIF

Stenciled Blueberry This simple
stencil motif can be used to brighten up a wall of plain
tiles anywhere in the house.

Order of work

1 Transfer the design to stencil card and carefully
cut it out.

2 Use masking tape to fix the stencil in place
over a commercially bought, ready-glazed tile,
then use a stencil brush to stipple in a selection of
tile paints.

3 Remove the stencil and seal the surface of
the tile.

You will need
- Stencil card
- Craft knife
- Masking tape
- Selection of tile paints
- Stencil brush
- Surface sealant
- Paintbrush
- Pre-glazed tile

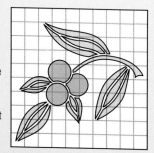

Arranging tiles
Use the stencil to add random detail to a wall of
plain tiles.

DESIGN IDEA

TECHNIQUE

DIFFICULTY

see also transferring motifs **53**

MOTIF

Chillies, Pepper, and Lemon

Real vegetables and fruit were used to make the molds for these tiles, but if you do not have access to these they can easily be modeled for the same effect.

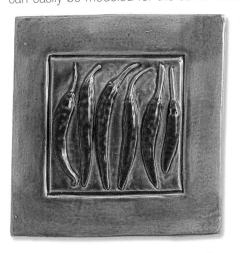

CLAY White earthenware fired to 2,012°F (1,100°C) biscuit and 1,868°F (1020°C) glaze

Order of work

1 Make the models for the tiles by either pressing sections of real fruits and vegetables into a clay tile or by modeling the details then casting in plaster to make a mold.

2 Make the tile by rolling a slab of clay and pressing it into the plaster mold.

3 After biscuit firing, apply the appropriate colored commercial paint-on glazes to the different areas of the tiles and fire to the required glaze temperature.

You will need

- White earthenware clay
- Plaster
- Selection of commercial paint-on glazes
- Paintbrushes

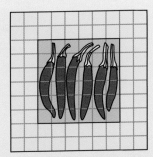

Arranging tiles

These tiles are meant to fit randomly into a scheme of plain tiles, along with other motifs of a similar subject matter.

DESIGN IDEAS

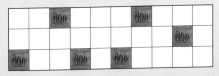

TECHNIQUE

DIFFICULTY

see also kilns and firing **18–21** mold making **22–23** drying tiles **37**

MOTIF

MOTIF

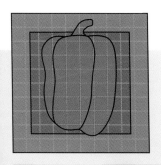

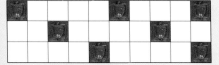

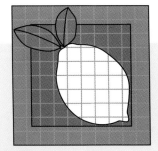

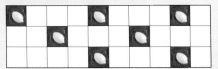

MOTIF

Apples
The paper resist technique is used as a stencil for this example, because only the area surrounding the apples is resisted.

CLAY Red earthenware fired to 2,012°F (1,100°C) biscuit and 1,976°F (1,080°C) glaze

Order of work

1 Apply a base coat of slip to a leather-hard tile, then cut a newspaper stencil for the apples and a second one for the leaf.

2 Dampen the apple stencil and position it over the tile, then sponge in the apple slip colors.

3 Lift the apple motif and position the leaf resist, then sponge in the leaf slip colors.

4 Sgraffito in the detail and biscuit fire, then apply a transparent glaze and fire to the recommended temperature.

You will need
- Red earthenware clay
- Selection of colored slips
- Newspaper
- Natural sponge
- Sgraffito tool
- Transparent earthenware glaze

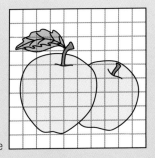

Arranging tiles
Position this tile with others of the same theme and style.

DESIGN IDEA

TECHNIQUE

DIFFICULTY

1

see also kilns and firing **18–21** applying slip **32** drying tiles **37** transferring motifs **53**

Fungi This is a really easy tile to make, and the motif is especially eye-catching in black and white.

Order of work

1 Apply a base coat of black slip to a leather-hard tile.

2 Transfer the design to the tile and sgraffito the outline of the motif followed by the pattern around the border.

3 After biscuit firing, apply a transparent glaze and fire to the appropriate temperature.

CLAY White earthenware fired to 2,012°F (1,100°C) biscuit and 1,976°F (1,080°C) glaze

You will need
• White earthenware clay
• Black slip
• Paintbrushes
• Sgraffito tool
• Transparent earthenware glaze

Arranging tiles
Combine this and other tiles made in the same style to form a panel, as a feature in a wall of otherwise plain tiles.

DESIGN IDEA

TECHNIQUE

DIFFICULTY

see also kilns and firing **18–21** applying slip **32** drying tiles **37** transferring motifs **53**

MOTIF 91

Garlic This tile would look great in a country kitchen, unless of course you don't like garlic!

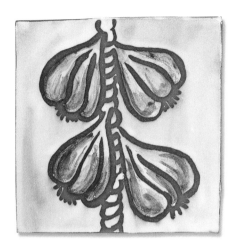

CLAY Red earthenware fired to 2,012°F (1,100°C) biscuit and 1,976°F (1,080°C) glaze

Order of work

1 Transfer the design to the surface of a biscuit-fired tile.

2 Wax the outline of the motif using a fine paintbrush.

3 Apply a white tin glaze, then paint in the detail with underglaze stains and fire to the appropriate temperature.

You will need
- Red earthenware clay
- Wax emulsion
- Fine paintbrush
- White tin glaze
- Selection of underglaze stains

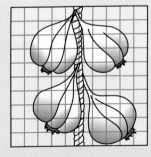

Arranging tiles
This tile would work well as a feature in a scheme of plain tiles, or it could be arranged vertically to look like a long rope of garlic.

DESIGN IDEAS

TECHNIQUE

DIFFICULTY

see also kilns and firing **18–21** drying tiles **37** wax resist **46** transferring motifs **53**

Sgraffito Pear

You could make tiles with the same background detail but without the motif, to intersperse with this tile and other fruit motifs for a really unique effect.

CLAY Red earthenware fired to 2,012°F (1,100°C) biscuit and 1,976°F (1,080°C) glaze

Order of work

1 Prepare the tile and allow it to dry to leather hard.

2 Transfer the design to the surface of the tile and sgraffito the motif using a sgraffito tool, and the background detail using a loop tool.

3 After biscuit firing, apply white tin glaze to the tile then wipe it back until it only remains in the sgraffito areas. Fire to the recommended glaze temperature.

You will need
- Red earthenware clay
- Sgraffito tool
- Loop tool
- White tin glaze

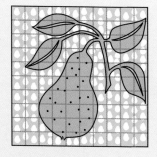

Arranging tiles
Randomly arrange these tiles within a scheme of plain tiles with the same background detail.

DESIGN IDEA

TECHNIQUE

DIFFICULTY

see also kilns and firing **18–21** drying tiles **37** transferring motifs **53**

MOTIF

93

Lemon, Peach, and Pear

These lively, painterly motifs require a freehand style to achieve the look, so you may like to practice on paper before committing yourself to the tile.

CLAY Red earthenware fired to 2,012°F (1,100°C) biscuit and 1,976°F (1,080°C) glaze

Order of work

1 Apply a base coat of white slip to a leather-hard clay tile and allow to dry out completely.

2 Transfer the design to the surface of the tile, then loosely paint in the background color using an underglaze stain, and complete the outline with black underglaze stain.

3 After biscuit firing, apply a transparent glaze and fire to the required temperature.

You will need
- Red earthenware clay
- White slip
- Paintbrushes
- Selection of underglaze stains, including black
- Transparent earthenware glaze

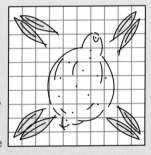

Arranging tiles
These tiles form a lovely repeat scheme for a kitchen wall, or work equally well as a border for plain tiles.

DESIGN IDEAS

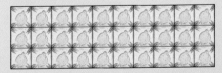

TECHNIQUE

DIFFICULTY

see also kilns and firing **18–21** applying slip **32** drying tiles **37** underglaze painting **43** transferring motifs **53**

MOTIF

MOTIF

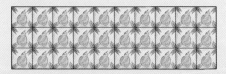

MOTIF

 96

Rattle
The nursery is an improbable room for tiled walls, however, the potential to create a visually exciting environment for the child using tiles is immense. Use these tiles on their own or team them together using complementary colors.

CLAY Red earthenware fired to 2,012°F (1,100°C) biscuit and 1,976°F (1,080°C) glaze

Order of work

1 Prepare the tile and allow to dry to the leather-hard stage.

2 Transfer the design to the surface of the tile then sgraffito the outline into the clay.

3 Using a selection of colored slips, fill in the sgraffito lines, then, when the slip is dry enough to work with, use a metal kidney to scrape it back to reveal the outline below.

4 After biscuit firing, cover the tile with transparent glaze and fire to the necessary temperature.

You will need
• Red earthenware clay
• Sgraffito tool
• Selection of colored slips
• Paintbrushes
• Metal kidney
• Transparent earthenware glaze

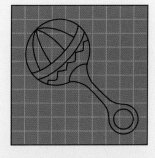

Arranging tiles
This tile would form a random repeat in a scheme of plain tiles or with other tiles of a similar style. Alternatively, it could be framed and hung as an artwork.

DESIGN IDEA

TECHNIQUE

DIFFICULTY

 1 2

see also kilns and firing **18–21** drying tiles **37** transferring motifs **53**

MOTIF

Teddy

Teddy bears are enduringly loved toys, so a section on nursery motifs would not be complete without one. This teddy is very easy to produce, and could be made in any number of color combinations, if you want to use it in repeat.

Order of work

1 Apply a base coat of colored slip to the surface of a leather-hard tile.

2 Cut out a newspaper teddy bear and fix it onto the surface of the tile with water, then lightly sponge over a second, contrasting slip color.

3 Remove the paper resist, then carefully transfer the detail of the teddy onto the tile and sgraffito the lines to reveal the clay color underneath.

4 After biscuit firing, cover the tile with transparent glaze and fire to the recommended temperature.

CLAY Red earthenware fired to 2,012°F (1,100°C) biscuit and 1,976°F (1,080°C) glaze

You will need

- Red earthenware clay
- Selection of colored slips
- Paintbrushes
- Newspaper
- Natural sponge
- Sgraffito tool
- Transparent earthenware glaze

Arranging tiles

This tile could be used as a random feature in a scheme of plain tiles, or, if made in different colorways, would look good as a border repeat.

DESIGN IDEA

TECHNIQUE

DIFFICULTY

 1

see also kilns and firing **18–21** drying tiles **37** transferring motifs **53**

MOTIF

98

Socks Brush-on commercial glazes, which are available in a myriad of color choices, are very easy to apply, and the perfect choice with which to decorate this very simple tile, which can be quickly made.

CLAY White earthenware fired to 2,012°F (1,100°C) biscuit and 1,868°F (1,020°C) glaze

Order of work

1 Prepare the tile and dry to leather hard.

2 Transfer the motif to the surface of the tile and use a fine tool to sgraffito the outline.

3 After biscuit firing the tile, paint in the different sections of the socks using a selection of paint-on glaze colors, and fire to the required temperature.

You will need
- White earthenware clay
- Fine sgraffito tool
- Selection of commercial paint-on glazes
- Paintbrushes

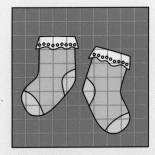

Arranging tiles
This tile is designed to form a random feature in a scheme of plain tiles.

DESIGN IDEA

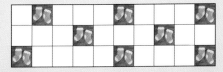

TECHNIQUE

DIFFICULTY

see also kilns and firing **18–21** drying tiles **37** transferring motifs **53**

MOTIF

Baby Carriage This is quite an
old-fashioned design of baby carriage, but much more
charming to look at than modern varieties, which would not work
quite so well as a motif.

Order of work

1 Prepare the tile and dry to leather hard.

2 Transfer the motif to the surface of the tile and sgraffito the outline.

3 After biscuit firing, apply a colored transparent glaze and wipe it back until it only remains in the sgraffito outline. Fire to glaze temperature.

CLAY White earthenware fired to 2,012°F (1,100°C) biscuit and 1,976°F (1,080°C) glaze

You will need
• White earthenware clay
• Sgraffito tool
• Colored transparent earthenware glaze

Arranging tiles
This tile would look most effective randomly placed with other tiles made in the same way, but utilizing different motifs and colorways.

DESIGN IDEA

TECHNIQUE

DIFFICULTY

see also kilns and firing **18–21** drying tiles **37** transferring motifs **53**

Motif directory

MOTIF

Ducky

Ducky was so named by my daughter, who very kindly helped in the making of many of the tiles in this book—she is 23 years old but thought the name sounded better than just "Duck."

CLAY White earthenware fired to 2,012°F (1,100°C) biscuit and 1,868°F (1,020°C) glaze

Order of work

1 Cut out the body of the duck from textured wallpaper, excluding the beak and eye and wing detail.

2 Roll the textured template onto a slab of soft clay then cut the tile to the correct size.

3 Remove the paper body and sgraffito the outline of the beak.

4 After biscuit firing, paint the duck and background using a selection of paint-on glazes and fire to the recommended temperature.

You will need

- Textured wallpaper
- White earthenware clay
- Rolling pin and roller guides
- Sgraffito tool
- Commercial paint-on glazes
- Paintbrushes

Arranging tiles

Although this tile is designed as a random motif, it would also look very good as a border if made in varying colorways.

DESIGN IDEA

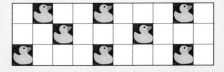

TECHNIQUE

DIFFICULTY

see also kilns and firing **18–21** drying tiles **37**

Train

Train This very colorful little scene is simply painted onto a commercially glazed tile, on a wall, using enamel colors, but could just as easily be painted onto a single glazed tile before it is laid in place.

Order of work

1 Transfer the outline of the motif to the surface of a tile on the wall.

2 Paint in the detail of the motif using a selection of enamel colors. It helps to paint one color at a time, allowing each to dry before painting subsequent colors.

3 When the enamel paint is dry, spray the surface with a suitable sealant.

You will need

- Paintbrushes
- Enamel colors
- Surface sealant

Arranging tiles

This tile is designed to form a random feature in a scheme of plain tiles, but if scaled up would look very good as a view-through-a-window mural, covering several tiles.

DESIGN IDEA

TECHNIQUE

DIFFICULTY

1

see also transferring motifs **53**

MOTIF

Balloons
This is a very simple motif that will quickly liven up a scheme of plain tiles. Try it in lots of different colorways.

Order of work

1 Transfer the design to stencil card and carefully cut out the motif.

2 Spray a little repositioning glue on the back of the stencil and secure it over the tile on the wall. Apply the tile paints following any of the stenciling methods.

3 Carefully remove the stencil and seal the surface of the tile.

You will need
- Stencil card and a sharp craft knife
- Repositioning spray glue
- Selection of tile paints
- Natural sponge or stencil brush
- Surface sealant

Arranging tiles

This motif looks especially jolly when randomly repeated in different colorways within a scheme of plain tiles.

DESIGN IDEA

🎈			🎈		🎈
	🎈			🎈	
🎈			🎈		🎈

TECHNIQUE

DIFFICULTY

 1

see also transferring motifs **53**

MOTIF

Flying Kite

This brightly colored tile is especially useful in that it would suit a room for either a girl or a boy.

CLAY Red earthenware fired to 2,012°F (1,100°C) biscuit and 1,976°F (1,080°C) glaze

Order of work

1 Apply a coat of white tin glaze to the surface of a biscuit-fired tile, then carefully transfer the outline of the design.

2 Use wax emulsion to mask out the clouds and paint in the colors of the kite and sails using underglaze stains.

3 Wax over the colored areas of the kite and paint over the whole tile with a thin wash of blue underglaze stain.

4 Finally, paint in the outline of the kite and sails in black underglaze stain and fire to glaze temperature.

You will need
- Red earthenware clay
- White earthenware tin glaze
- Paintbrushes
- Wax emulsion
- Selection of underglaze stains

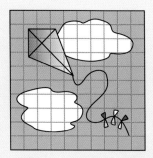

Arranging tiles

This motif is designed to be randomly positioned in a scheme of plain tiles, but if scaled up would look very good as a mural over a larger area.

DESIGN IDEA

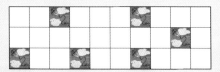

TECHNIQUE

DIFFICULTY

see also kilns and firing **18–21** drying tiles **37** wax resist **46** transferring motifs **53**

MOTIF

Doll
This little doll is painted in a free style that looks simple, but actually demands some practice to get right. Try painting her on sheets of paper until you are confident enough to commit to the clay.

CLAY Red earthenware fired to 2,012°F (1,100°C) biscuit and 1,976°F (1,080°C) glaze

Order of work

1 Apply a base coat of white slip to the surface of a leather-hard tile and allow to dry.

2 Transfer the outline detail of the motif onto the tile then paint in the colors using a selection of underglaze stains.

3 After biscuit firing, apply transparent glaze and fire to the necessary temperature.

You will need
- Red earthenware clay
- White slip
- Paintbrushes
- Selection of underglaze stains
- Transparent earthenware glaze

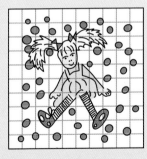

Arranging tiles
This tile could be repeated in different colorways and positioned randomly in a scheme of otherwise plain tiles.

DESIGN IDEA

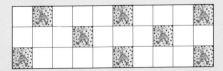

TECHNIQUE

DIFFICULTY

see also kilns and firing **18–21** drying tiles **37** underglaze painting **43** wax resist **46** transferring motifs **53**

MOTIF

Cubes
The design of this tile is based on children's building bricks, but the bricks have been painted very loosely, making the tile suitable for any number of locations, not just the nursery.

CLAY Red earthenware fired to 2,012°F (1,100°C) biscuit and 1,976°F (1,080°C) glaze

Order of work

1 Apply a base coat of white slip to the surface of a leather-hard tile and allow to dry.

2 Transfer the outline detail of the motif onto the tile then paint in the colors using a selection of underglaze stains.

3 After biscuit firing, apply transparent glaze and fire to glaze temperature.

You will need
- Red earthenware clay
- White slip
- Paintbrushes
- Selection of underglaze stains
- Transparent earthenware glaze

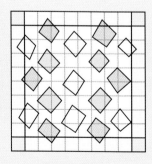

Arranging tiles
This tile could be repeated in different colorways.

DESIGN IDEA

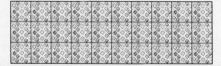

TECHNIQUE

DIFFICULTY

see also kilns and firing **18–21** drying tiles **37** underglaze painting **43** wax resist **46** transferring motifs **53**

MOTIF

106

Stone Spiral This design is loosely based on a stone spiral staircase designed by Antonio Gaudi in Barcelona.

CLAY Porcelain fired to 1,832ºF (1,000ºC) biscuit and 2,300ºF (1,260ºC) glaze

Order of work

1 Prepare the tile and dry to leather hard.

2 Paint a very even coat of black body stain onto a nonabsorbent board and allow to dry.

3 Trace the design onto a sheet of paper then position the sheet over the body stain and draw over the design.

4 Carefully lay the monoprint sheet on the surface of the tile and gently smooth over with a finger to transfer the design. After biscuit firing, apply transparent glaze and fire to the required temperature.

You will need

- Porcelain clay
- Black body stain
- Paintbrushes
- Paper and pencil
- Transparent stoneware glaze

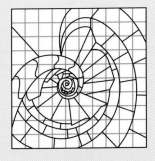

Arranging tiles

This tile could be positioned randomly in a scheme of plain tiles, or used in full repeat, or as a border.

DESIGN IDEAS

TECHNIQUE

DIFFICULTY

see also kilns and firing **18–21** drying tiles **37** transferring motifs **53**

MOTIF

Windows

This motif takes the form of an abstracted view through archways to the windows beyond, and is achieved using the majolica technique.

CLAY Red earthenware fired to 2,012°F (1,100°C) biscuit and 1,976°F (1,080°C) glaze

Order of work

1 Apply a coat of white tin glaze to the surface of a biscuit-fired tile then carefully transfer the outline of the design to the tile.

2 Cut a newspaper stencil to cover the area around the archways and fix it onto the surface of the tile with a little water.

3 Paint over the archway areas with a thin wash of underglaze stain, then lightly accent sponge half of each archway in another, complementary, stain.

4 Using a fine brush, outline the detail of the motif with black underglaze stain, then fire to glaze temperature.

You will need

- Red earthenware clay
- White earthenware tin glaze
- Fine paintbrush
- Newspaper
- Selection of underglaze stains
- Natural sponge

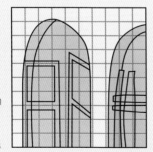

Arranging tiles

This motif is designed to be randomly positioned in a scheme of plain tiles, but if scaled up would look very good as a mural over a larger area.

DESIGN IDEA

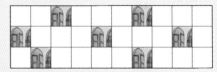

TECHNIQUE

DIFFICULTY

see also kilns and firing **18–21** drying tiles **37**

MOTIF

108 Corbel

Corbels are designed to fit in an angle within a building, often appearing to support a structure such as a ceiling, but they are generally only decorative architectural details. Here they are made in low relief to retain some suggestion of their original use.

CLAY Stoneware casting slip fired to 1,832°F (1,000°C) biscuit and 2,300°F (1,260°C) glaze

Order of work

1 Roll a thick tile—approximately ¾ in. (1.5 cm) thick—and transfer the design to its surface.

2 Carve out the detail of the design to form a low relief, making sure you do not create any undercuts.

3 Cast the model in plaster, then, when the mold is dry, cast the tile using stoneware casting slip.

4 After biscuit firing, paint over the surface of the tile with copper oxide, then wipe it back a little and cover with reactive or opaque glaze. Fire to glaze temperature.

You will need

- Modeling tool
- Potter's plaster
- Stoneware casting slip
- Copper oxide
- Paintbrushes
- Stoneware glaze, reactive white or opaque

Arranging tiles

To make the tile repeat exactly you will need to make another mold as a mirror image of this one, and use both.

DESIGN IDEAS

TECHNIQUE

DIFFICULTY

see also kilns and firing **18–21** mold making **22–23** drying tiles **37** oxide decoration **45–47** transferring motifs **53**

Ironwork

Old ironwork railings are a great source of inspiration for tile design, and the slip-trailing technique a perfect way to represent them. You may need to practice a little before trailing onto the tile, but otherwise this is a very easy effect to create.

Order of work

1 Transfer the design to the surface of a dry, unfired tile.

2 Carefully slip trail the outline in black.

3 After biscuit firing, apply a base coat of transparent colored glaze, then lightly sponge over using a second color—green and blue work very well. Fire the tile to glaze temperature.

CLAY White earthenware fired to 2,012ºF (1,100ºC) biscuit and 1,976ºF (1,080ºC) glaze

You will need

- White earthenware clay
- Black slip
- Slip trailer
- Two colored transparent earthenware glazes
- Natural sponge

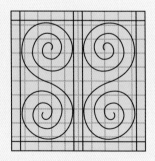

Arranging tiles

This tile forms a good repeat, and would look good as a border or column frame.

DESIGN IDEA

TECHNIQUE

DIFFICULTY

see also kilns and firing **18–21** drying tiles **37** transferring motifs **53**

MOTIF

110

Doorway

Entrances and doorways are often architectural focal points in a building. This doorway is in the classical style, with columns on both sides and an archway over the top. It is a simple tile to make using two glazes to accent the detail.

CLAY White stoneware fired to 1,832°F (1,000°C) biscuit and 2,300°F (1,260°C) glaze

Order of work

1 Prepare the tile and allow it to dry to leather hard.

2 Transfer the design to the surface of the tile and finely sgraffito or carve out the detail of the motif.

3 After biscuit firing, apply black glaze to the surface of the tile, then wipe it back so that it only remains in the carved lines.

4 Apply a second coat of pale colored transparent glaze to the tile, and fire to glaze temperature.

You will need
- White stoneware clay
- Sgraffito or modeling tool
- Black stoneware glaze
- Pale colored transparent stoneware glaze

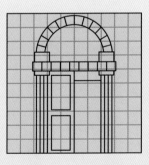

Arranging tiles
This tile would make a very good border repeat.

DESIGN IDEA

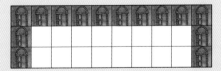

TECHNIQUE

DIFFICULTY

see also kilns and firing **18–21** drying tiles **37** transferring motifs **53**

MOTIF

Columns
Columns feature widely in classical architecture and make a good motif for repeat tiles.

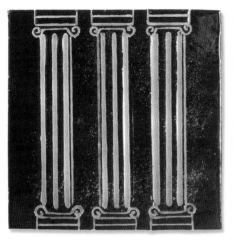

CLAY White earthenware fired to 2,012°F (1,100°C) biscuit and 1,976°F (1,080°C) glaze

Order of work

1 Apply a base coat of colored slip to the surface of a leather-hard tile and allow to dry to the touch.

2 Transfer the design to the surface of the tile then sgraffito the detail, varying the thickness of the lines on the columns. A fine loop tool may work best for this. The clay should be visible through the lines.

3 After biscuit firing, apply a transparent colored glaze and fire to glaze temperature.

You will need
- White earthenware clay
- Colored slip
- Paintbrushes
- Sgraffito tool
- Fine-ended loop tool (optional)
- Colored transparent earthenware glaze

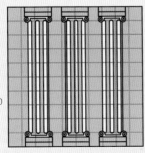

Arranging tiles
This tile would make a great border or column repeat to frame a plain scheme of tiles.

DESIGN IDEA

TECHNIQUE

DIFFICULTY

see also kilns and firing **18–21** applying slip **32** drying tiles **37** transferring motifs **53**

MOTIF

112

Castle

This tile uses the Raku technique of firing to achieve the strong contrast of black and white, but a similar effect could be achieved with black and white glaze if you do not have a Raku kiln.

CLAY Grogged white Raku clay fired to 1,832°F (1,000°C) biscuit and approximately 1,652°F (900°C) Raku glaze with a smoke reduction

Order of work

1 Prepare the tile and allow it to dry to leather hard.

2 Transfer the design to the surface of the tile and sgraffito the detail.

3 After biscuit firing, wax out the areas of the tile that are to be black: the windows and area beyond the battlement and the sgraffito lines.

4 Apply a coat of transparent Raku glaze to the tile then Raku fire and reduce in sawdust to achieve the black smoked areas. Clean the tile with water and a scouring pad to remove smoke marks on the glaze.

You will need

- Raku clay
- Sgraffito tool
- Wax emulsion
- Paintbrushes
- Transparent Raku glaze
- Scouring pad

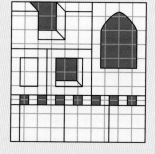

Arranging tiles

This tile could be used randomly as a feature in a scheme of plain tiles, or in repeat where it would make an interesting pattern.

DESIGN IDEAS

TECHNIQUE

DIFFICULTY

see also kilns and firing **18–21** raku firing **21** drying tiles **37** wax resist **46** transferring motifs **53**

Grid Plan

The idea for this tile was taken from a grid plan of buildings, and looks quite abstract in completion. It is a difficult tile to make in that it requires cutting out a lot of textured wallpaper, but once you have done this the rest is easy.

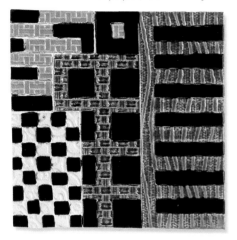

CLAY White earthenware fired to 2,012°F (1,100°C) biscuit and 1,868°F (1,020°C) glaze

Order of work

1 Cut out textured wallpaper stencils for each of the five sections of the motif as represented in the tile.

2 Position the stencils over a prepared tile and carefully roll them into the surface. Remove the wallpaper and cut the tile back to shape if it has distorted.

3 After biscuit firing, brush black paint-on glaze over all the untextured areas of the tile, then fill in the other colors accordingly and fire to the required temperature.

You will need

- Selection of textured wallpapers
- White earthenware clay
- Rolling pin and roller guides
- Commercial paint-on glazes
- Paintbrushes

Arranging tiles

This tile will form a very colorful full repeat.

DESIGN IDEA

TECHNIQUE

DIFFICULTY

see also kilns and firing **18–21** drying tiles **37** transferring motifs **53**

Church Windows

Churches are beautiful buildings that provide a wealth of inspiration for the artist. With this motif window detailing has been simply but effectively recreated using very basic techniques.

CLAY Porcelain fired to 1,832°F (1,000°C) biscuit and 2,300°F (1,260°C) glaze

Order of work

1 Prepare the tile and dry to leather hard.

2 Transfer the design to the surface of the tile and sgraffito the detail.

3 After biscuit firing, cover the tile with glaze and wipe back so that it mostly rests in the sgraffito detail, with some remaining on the stonework, to give an aged look. Fire the tile to glaze temperature.

You will need
- Porcelain clay
- Sgraffito tool
- Dark stoneware glaze
- Paintbrush

Arranging tiles
This tile could be used as a random feature in a scheme of plain tiles, or in repeat.

DESIGN IDEAS

TECHNIQUE

DIFFICULTY

see also kilns and firing **18–21** drying tiles **37** transferring motifs **53**

MOTIF

Dome
The dome of this building is set at an angle to create a wonderful pattern, which could be used to form a very colorful repeat.

Order of work

1 Prepare the tile and allow to dry to the leather-hard stage.

2 Transfer the design to the surface of the tile and sgraffito the detail.

3 After biscuit firing, apply a transparent glaze and fire to glaze temperature.

4 Paint a thin and even wash of each of the luster colors onto the tile and fire to luster temperature.

CLAY Porcelain fired to 1,832°F (1,000°C) biscuit and 2,300°F (1,260°C) glaze. Luster firing to 1,346°F (730°C)

You will need
- Porcelain clay
- Sgraffito tool
- Transparent glaze
- Paintbrushes
- Selection of luster colors

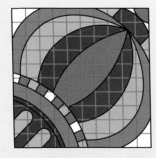

Arranging tiles
This tile could be used as a random feature in a scheme of plain tiles, or as a very colorful repeat of four, rotated to create a circular pattern.

DESIGN IDEAS

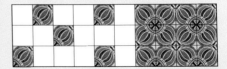

TECHNIQUE

DIFFICULTY

see also kilns and firing **18–21** drying tiles **37** transferring motifs **53**

MOTIF

Garden Urn
The most difficult part of making this tile is cutting out the lino block, but once you have done this successfully you will be able to make any number of tiles in this style.

CLAY White stoneware fired to 1,832°F (1,000°C) biscuit and 2,300°F (1,260°C) glaze

Order of work

1 Transfer the design to the surface of a lino block and carefully cut it out using a range of cutting tools.

2 Roll out a slab of clay and roll the lino block over the surface to impress the design.

3 Remove the lino block and cut the tile to size.

4 After biscuit firing, brush a copper oxide wash over the raised detail and wipe back a little, before covering with reactive or opaque glaze and refiring to glaze temperature.

You will need
- 6-in. (15-cm) square lino block
- Lino-cutting tool
- White stoneware clay
- Copper oxide
- Stoneware glaze
- Reactive glaze

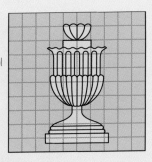

Arranging tiles
This tile is designed to form a random repeat in a scheme of plain tiles, but could be used in repeat to form a border or frame.

DESIGN IDEAS

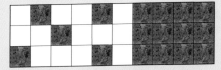

TECHNIQUE

DIFFICULTY

see also kilns and firing **18–21** drying tiles **37** oxide decoration **45–47** transferring motifs **53**

MOTIF

Stonework
Decorative stone masonry lends itself well to interpretation in sprig form, and in this tile a very simple sprig has been made to form the relief detail in the center of the tile.

CLAY White earthenware fired to 2,012ºF (1,100ºC) biscuit and 1,976ºF (1,080ºC) glaze

Order of work

1 Make a sprig mold for one of the central motifs in the tile.

2 Transfer the motif to the surface of a leather-hard tile, then sgraffito the wall detail surrounding the sprig and fill in the lines with colored slip.

3 When the slip has dried off sufficiently, use a metal kidney to scrape the excess away to reveal the pattern below, then carefully fix the four sprigs into place in the center using a toothbrush and water to score the underside and corresponding position on the tile.

4 After biscuit firing, cover with colored transparent glaze and fire to the recommended temperature.

You will need
- Potter's plaster
- White earthenware clay
- Sgraffito tool
- Colored slip
- Paintbrush
- Metal kidney
- Toothbrush
- Transparent earthenware glaze

Arranging tiles
This tile would make a good border repeat in a scheme of plain tiles.

DESIGN IDEA

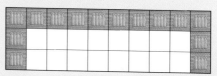

TECHNIQUE

DIFFICULTY

see also kilns and firing **18–21** making sprig molds **24–25** drying tiles **37** transferring motifs **53**

Motif directory

Church
The very simple outline of this church makes an easy stencil to cut out and complete.

Order of work

1 Transfer the design to stencil card and carefully cut out the motif.

2 Spray a little repositioning glue on the back of the stencil and secure it over the tile on the wall. Apply tile paints following any of the stenciling methods.

3 Carefully remove the stencil then lightly sponge a very pale color around the church.

4 Seal the surface of the tile.

You will need
- Stencil card and a sharp craft knife
- Repositioning spray glue
- Selection of tile paints
- Natural sponge or stencil brush
- Surface sealant

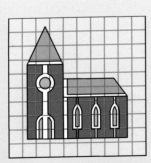

Arranging tiles
This motif looks especially effective when randomly repeated in different colorways within a scheme of plain tiles.

DESIGN IDEA

TECHNIQUE

DIFFICULTY

1

MOTIF

119 Minaret

The minaret featured on this tile has been abstracted a little to make it more decorative. You could try making it in different colorways for added interest.

Order of work

1 Make a sprig mold of the minaret.

2 Fix the sprig onto the surface of a leather-hard tile using a toothbrush and water to score the underside and the relevant position on the tile. Make sure no air is trapped beneath the sprig, otherwise it will blow off in the firing.

3 After biscuit firing, paint a copper oxide wash over the sprig and wipe back a little, then cover the tile with white tin glaze and fire to glaze temperature.

CLAY White stoneware fired to 1,832°F (1,000°C) biscuit and 2,300°F (1,260°C) glaze

You will need

- Potter's plaster
- White stoneware clay
- Copper oxide
- Paintbrushes
- Toothbrush
- White stoneware tin glaze

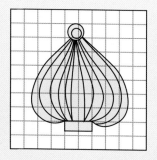

Arranging tiles

This tile would look equally good either randomly positioned in a scheme of plain tiles or in repeat, either as a border or complete.

DESIGN IDEAS

TECHNIQUE

DIFFICULTY

see also kilns and firing **18–21** making sprig molds **24–25** drying tiles **37** oxide decoration **45–47** transferring motifs **53**

MOTIF

Aztec Serpent

The impressing and Raku techniques used to decorate this tile effectively interpret the original artifact, which was made in turquoise mosaic and probably worn as a brooch or chest ornament.

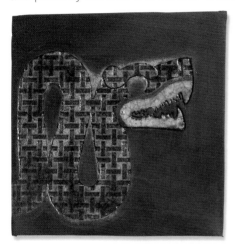

CLAY Grogged white Raku clay fired to 1,832°F (1,000°C) biscuit and approximately 1,652°F (900°C) Raku glaze with a smoke reduction

Order of work

1 Cut out the main part of the serpent's body, excluding the jaw, from textured wallpaper.

2 Position the wallpaper shape over a prepared tile, textured side down, then roll it onto the surface. Remove the wallpaper and cut the tile back to shape if it has distorted.

3 Transfer the detail of the jaw to the tile and finely sgraffito it in.

4 After biscuit firing, paint turquoise Raku glaze over the body of the serpent and transparent Raku glaze over the jaw and teeth. Raku fire and reduce the tile in sawdust to create the black, smoked background of the motif, then clean off the smoke marks from the glazed surface of the tile with water and a scouring pad.

You will need

- Textured wallpaper
- White Raku clay
- Sgrafitto tool
- Paintbrushes
- Transparent Raku glaze
- Scouring pad

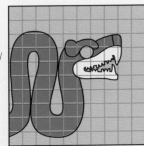

Arranging tiles

Make a left and right version of this tile, as the serpent is meant to be double ended. They will form a dramatic border repeat for plain tiles in the same turquoise color.

DESIGN IDEA

TECHNIQUE

DIFFICULTY

see also kilns and firing **18–21** raku firing **21** drying tiles **37** transferring motifs **53**

Greek Pattern with Border

121

The ancient Greeks were masters in the arts, evidence of which remains in their architecture and ceramics, from where this motif has been drawn from.

Culture

122

CLAY Red earthenware fired to 2,012°F (1,100°C) biscuit and 1,976°F (1,080°C) glaze

Order of work

1 Apply a base coat of white slip to the surface of a leather-hard tile, then allow to dry completely.

2 Paint over the whole tile with a thin wash of yellow ocher underglaze stain. Transfer the motif to the surface of the tile and use black underglaze stain to paint in the detail of the design.

3 After biscuit firing, apply transparent glaze and fire to the recommended temperature.

You will need
• Red earthenware clay
• White slip
• Paintbrushes
• Underglaze stains
• Transparent earthenware glaze

Arranging tiles
This tile would form a good repeat with the border tile, or could be used randomly in a plain scheme with the border tile as a framing device.

DESIGN IDEAS

TECHNIQUE

DIFFICULTY

1 **2**

see also kilns and firing **18–21** applying slip **32** drying tiles **37** underglaze painting **43** transferring motifs **53**

MOTIF

North American Indian Face

The face features widely in North American traditional art, with masks playing an important role in tribal culture. Often the faces seem grotesque but have spiritual significance associated with the deities.

CLAY Red earthenware fired to 2,012°F (1,100°C) biscuit and 1,976°F (1,080°C) glaze

Order of work

1 Apply a base coat of white slip to the surface of a leather-hard tile and allow to dry completely.

2 Paint over the whole tile with a thin wash of underglaze stain.

3 Transfer the motif to the surface of the tile and paint black underglaze stain in the detail.

4 After biscuit firing, apply transparent glaze and fire to glaze temperature.

You will need

- Red earthenware clay
- White slip
- Paintbrushes
- Two underglaze stains, including black
- Transparent earthenware glaze

Arranging tiles

This tile can be used individually, as a framed artwork, or randomly positioned within a scheme of plain tiles.

DESIGN IDEA

TECHNIQUE

DIFFICULTY

see also kilns and firing **18–21** applying slip **32** drying tiles **37** underglaze painting **43** transferring motifs **53**

Buddha

Images of Buddha are always very popular, and this tile shows quite a beautiful and serene pose, finished off simply in glaze that picks up the detail of the face.

Culture

CLAY Porcelain fired to 1,832°F (1,000°C) biscuit and 2,300°F (1,260°C) glaze

Order of work

1 Prepare the tile and dry to leather hard.

2 Transfer the design to the surface of the tile and finely carve out the detail using a modeling or sgraffito tool.

3 After biscuit firing, apply a pale colored transparent glaze, allowing it to pool in the detail, and fire to the required temperature.

You will need

- Porcelain clay
- Modeling or sgraffito tool
- Pale colored transparent stoneware glaze
- Paintbrush

Arranging tiles

This is very much a feature tile, which looks most effective when framed as an artwork.

DESIGN IDEA

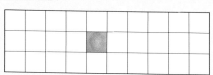

TECHNIQUE

DIFFICULTY

1 **2**

see also kilns and firing **18–21** drying tiles **37** transferring motifs **53**

MOTIF

125

Indian Textile The design for this tile was
inspired by textiles in this instance by the blocks
that are actually used to print the original textiles.

CLAY Red earthenware fired to 2,012°F (1,100°C)
biscuit and 1,976°F (1,080°C) glaze

Order of work

1 Apply a coat of white tin glaze to the surface
of a biscuit-fired tile, then transfer the design
to the surface of the tile.

2 Using cobalt oxide mixed in a small amount of
water, and a thin brush, carefully paint in the
outline of the motif.

3 Lightly sponge over the tile with a
complementary colored underglaze stain (yellow
was used here). Fire the tile to glaze temperature.

You will need

- Red
earthenware clay
- White
earthenware tin
glaze
- Cobalt oxide
- Fine paintbrush
- Natural sponge
- Colored
underglaze stain

Arranging tiles

This tile forms a complete repeat, and could be used
in any number of rooms in the home.

DESIGN IDEA

TECHNIQUE

DIFFICULTY

1 **2** **3**

see also kilns and firing **18–21** drying tiles **37** transferring motifs **53**

MOTIF

Indian Border This border pattern was copied from an Indian textile printing block, and made into a mold for quick repeats.

Order of work

1 Prepare the tile and allow it to dry to leather hard.

2 Transfer the design to the surface of the tile and carve out the pattern, taking care to avoid making undercuts.

3 Make a plaster mold of the tile, then, when the mold is dry, press a slab of soft clay into the mold to make the tile, making sure it is pressed well into the pattern detail.

4 After biscuit firing, glaze the tile using a colored transparent glaze to match the Indian textile tile shown opposite.

CLAY White earthenware fired to 2,012°F (1,100°C) biscuit and 1,976°F (1,080°C) glaze.

You will need
• Clay for the tile model
• Modeling tool
• Potter's plaster
• White earthenware clay
• Colored transparent earthenware glaze
• Paintbrush

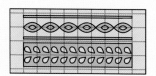

Arranging tiles
This tile forms a border repeat that is meant to work with the previous Indian textile tile.

DESIGN IDEA

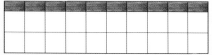

TECHNIQUE

DIFFICULTY

see also kilns and firing **18–21** applying slip **32** drying tiles **37** applying underglaze colors with shaped sponges **43** transferring motifs **53**

MOTIF

New Guinea Bark Cloth
The design for this tile is loosely inspired by the cloth made by the women of Lake Sentani in New Guinea. It is a much more colorful version than the actual cloths, which are made using earth colors.

Order of work

1 Transfer the outline of the design to the surface of a tile on the wall and paint on enamel colors one at a time, allowing each to dry before applying the next, to prevent the colors bleeding into one another.

2 When the enamels have dried, spray with surface sealant.

You will need

- Selection of on-glaze enamel colors, including black
- Paintbrushes
- Surface sealant

Arranging tiles

This tile can be randomly positioned within a scheme of plain tiles.

DESIGN IDEA

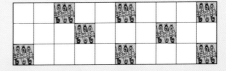

TECHNIQUE

DIFFICULTY

see also kilns and firing **18–21** drying tiles **37** transferring motifs **53**

Scandinavian Rock Painting

The inspiration for this tile was taken from Bronze Age Scandinavian rock paintings, originating *c.*3000 BCE.

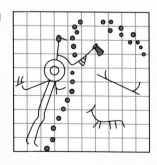

CLAY White stoneware fired to 1,832°F (1,000°C) biscuit and 2,300°F (1,260°C) glaze

Order of work

1 Prepare the tile and allow it to dry to leather hard.

2 Roughly texture the surface of the tile using scrunched-up aluminum foil, to give the impression of rock.

3 Transfer the design to the surface of the textured tile and carefully slip trail the outline detail of the motif using red slip.

4 After biscuit firing, apply a transparent glaze and fire to the required temperature.

You will need

- Aluminum foil
- Red slip
- Slip trailer
- Transparent stoneware glaze
- Paintbrush

Arranging tiles

This tile is designed to be a framed artwork.

DESIGN IDEA

see also kilns and firing **18–21** drying tiles **37** transferring motifs **53**

Motif directory

MOTIF

Egyptian Scarab and Lotus

A section on ethnic motifs would not be complete without reference to the ancient Egyptians, and this tile shows two popular symbols in one tile, the scarab and lotus flower.

CLAY Red earthenware fired to 2,012ºF (1,100ºC) biscuit and 1,976ºF (1,080ºC) glaze

Order of work

1 Prepare the tile and dry to leather hard.

2 Transfer the design to the surface of the tile and sgraffito the outline.

3 Working with one color at a time, fill in the sgraffito lines with a selection of colored slips, allowing each one to dry before filling in the next, to ensure no color bleeding occurs.

4 When all the slip colors have been filled in and the surface is dry enough, use a metal kidney to scrape away the excess to reveal the motif below.

5 After biscuit firing, apply a transparent glaze and fire to glaze temperature.

You will need
- Sgraffito tool
- Selection of colored slips
- Paintbrushes
- Metal kidney
- Transparent earthenware glaze

Arranging tiles

This tile could be used as a random feature in a scheme of plain tiles, or in repeats of four if the tile is rotated so that the lotus forms a central design.

DESIGN IDEAS

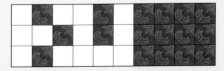

TECHNIQUE

DIFFICULTY

see also kilns and firing **18–21** drying tiles **37** transferring motifs **53**

188

MOTIF

130 Aboriginal Stone Drawing

This design is taken from an aboriginal *churinga* or inscribed stone. The stones were decorated with designs that were associated with the songs and stories of the spirits.

CLAY Red earthenware fired to 2,012°F (1,100°C) biscuit and 1,976°F (1,080°C) glaze

Order of work

1 Apply a base coat of colored slip to the surface of a leather-hard tile and allow to dry to the touch.

2 Transfer the design to the surface of the tile, then sgraffito the detail.

3 After biscuit firing, apply a colored transparent glaze and fire to the recommended glaze temperature.

You will need
- Red earthenware clay
- Colored slip
- Sgraffito tool
- Colored transparent earthenware glaze
- Paintbrush

Arranging tiles
This tile could be used either randomly in a scheme of plain tiles, or in repeat to fill a whole wall.

DESIGN IDEAS

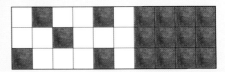

TECHNIQUE

DIFFICULTY

see also kilns and firing **18–21** applying slip **32** drying tiles **37** transferring motifs **53**

MOTIF

Flowers
This tile was not designed with flowers in mind, but was so named by my daughter, who immediately interpreted the swirled lines as such.

CLAY White earthenware fired to 2,012°F (1,100°C) biscuit and 1,976°F (1,080°C) glaze

Order of work

1 Prepare the tile and allow to dry to the leather-hard stage.

2 Transfer the swirled lines to the surface of the tile and slip trail them using black slip.

3 After biscuit firing, cover the surface of the tile with transparent glaze, then dip half the tile in a second colored transparent glaze, and again diagonally in a third glaze.

4 Make sure all the glaze is thoroughly cleaned off the back of the tile before firing to glaze temperature.

You will need
- White earthenware clay
- Black slip
- Slip trailer
- Transparent and colored earthenware glazes
- Paintbrush

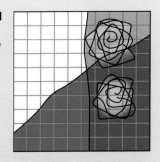

Arranging tiles
This tile would make a great random repeat in a scheme of plain white tiles

DESIGN IDEA

TECHNIQUE

DIFFICULTY **1 2**

see also kilns and firing **18–21** slip trailing **34** drying tiles **37** transferring motifs **53**

Water, Hills, and Trees

Finding titles for these abstract tiles has been difficult, and ultimately resolved by calling them by whatever springs to mind first, rather like a psychological test.

CLAY White earthenware fired to 2,012°F (1,100°C) biscuit and 1,976°F (1,080°C) glaze

Order of work

1 Cut out a tile-sized square of newspaper and use a craft knife to cut out the number 1 shape from the square. Dampen and attach the negative section of paper (the stencil) to the surface of the tile.

2 Sponge the first slip color over the exposed area of tile.

3 Work through the remainder of the numbered areas using newspaper resist stencils to mask off the areas of pattern, applying the black slip areas last.

4 After biscuit firing, apply a colored transparent glaze and fire to glaze temperature.

You will need

- Newspaper
- Craft knife
- White earthenware clay
- Colored slips,
- Natural sponge
- Colored transparent earthenware glaze

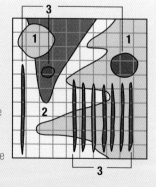

Arranging tiles

This tile is designed as an art tile, so would be best framed alone; however it would work as a random repeat in a scheme of plain tiles.

DESIGN IDEA

TECHNIQUE

DIFFICULTY

see also kilns and firing **18–21** applying slip **32** drying tiles **37** transferring motifs **53**

MOTIF

Abstract Block

This tile is very simple to make, but looks good because of the combination of colors. If you choose other colors for your tile make a test tile first, to make sure the colors work together and balance.

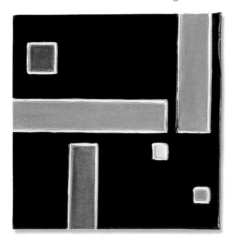

CLAY White earthenware fired to 2,012°F (1,100°C) biscuit and 1,868°F (1,020°C) glaze

Order of work

1 Prepare the tile and allow it to dry to leather hard.

2 Transfer the design to the surface of the tile and sgraffito the outline of the blocks.

3 After biscuit firing, paint the tile using a selection of commercial paint-on glazes, making sure the color combination balances. Fire to the recommended temperature.

You will need

- White earthenware clay
- Sgraffito tool
- Selection of commercial paint-on glazes
- Paintbrushes

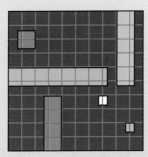

Arranging tiles

This tile could be used to form a great random repeat, perhaps turning the tiles in the arrangement so that the blocks lie at different angles.

DESIGN IDEA

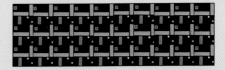

TECHNIQUE

DIFFICULTY

see also kilns and firing **18–21** drying tiles **37** transferring motifs **53**

MOTIF

Flow
This is a beautifully subtle tile that looks good in repeat. Try making it in different colorways for extra interest.

Abstract

Order of work

1 Prepare the tile and dry to leather hard.

2 Transfer the design to the surface of the tile and sgraffito the lines of the pattern.

3 Fill in the lines with colored slip then, when dry enough, scrape away the excess using a metal kidney, to reveal the design below.

4 After biscuit firing, apply a colored transparent glaze and fire to glaze temperature.

CLAY White earthenware fired to 2,012°F (1,100°C) biscuit and 1,976°F (1,080°C) glaze

You will need
- White earthenware clay
- Sgraffito tool
- Colored slip
- Paintbrushes
- Colored transparent earthenware glaze
- Metal kidney

Arranging tiles
This tile forms a complete repeat, but can be used as a border or column repeat.

DESIGN IDEA

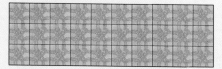

TECHNIQUE

DIFFICULTY

see also kilns and firing **18–21** drying tiles **37** transferring motifs **53**

MOTIF

Spiral and Dots
This tile requires a freehand approach to apply the oxide spiral, so try it out on paper until you feel confident enough to paint it onto the tile.

Order of work

1 Apply a coat of white tin glaze to the surface of a biscuit-fired tile, then dip each side of the tile in a colored transparent glaze to form a border. Clean off the back of the tile thoroughly.

2 Transfer the design to the surface of the glazed tile then, using a fine brush, carefully paint in the lines with a wash of copper oxide.

3 Splash a few dots of oxide over the tile before firing to glaze temperature.

CLAY Red earthenware fired to 2,012°F (1,100°C) biscuit and 1,976°F (1,080°C) glaze

You will need
- Red earthenware clay
- White tin glaze
- Colored transparent earthenware glaze
- Copper oxide
- Fine paintbrush

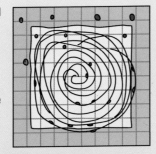

Arranging tiles
This tile is designed to form a random feature in a scheme of plain tiles, but could also be used as a border repeat.

DESIGN IDEA

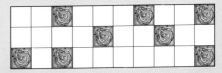

TECHNIQUE	DIFFICULTY

see also kilns and firing **18–21** drying tiles **37** oxide decoration **45–47** transferring motifs **53**

MOTIF

Diamond
This is an incredibly easy tile to make, with a rather retro look, making it ideal for any number of situations in the home.

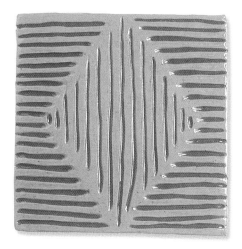

CLAY Red earthenware fired to 2,012°F (1,100°C) biscuit and 1,976°F (1,080°C) glaze

Order of work

1 Apply a base coat of colored slip to the surface of a leather-hard tile and allow to dry to the touch.

2 Transfer the design to the surface of the tile then sgraffito the lines using the end of a fine loop tool.

3 After biscuit firing, apply a colored transparent glaze to the surface and fire to glaze temperature.

You will need

- Red earthenware clay
- Colored slip
- Fine loop tool
- Colored transparent earthenware glaze
- Paintbrush

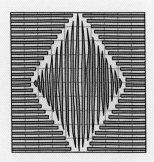

Arranging tiles
This tile can be used either randomly or in repeat, and would fit in any room in the home.

DESIGN IDEA

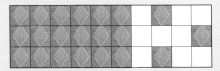

TECHNIQUE

DIFFICULTY

see also kilns and firing **18–21** applying slip **32** drying tiles **37** transferring motifs **53**

MOTIF

Chim's Pattern

This tile is named after a friend of mine who very kindly made it. It has a lovely clean and crisp quality, which would look good in a modern kitchen.

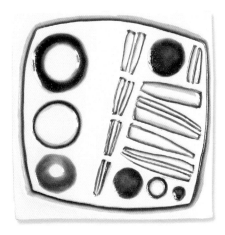

CLAY White earthenware fired to 2,012°F (1,100°C) biscuit and 1,976°F (1,080°C) glaze

Order of work

1 Prepare the tile and allow it to dry to leather hard.

2 Transfer the design to the surface of the tile and carve out the detail of the pattern, creating different levels and thickness of line.

3 After biscuit firing, apply a coat of colored transparent glaze then wipe it back so that it only remains in the detail. Fire to glaze temperature.

You will need
- White earthenware clay
- Modeling tool
- Colored transparent earthenware glaze
- Paintbrush

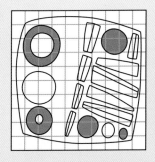

Arranging tiles

This tile would look good randomly placed in a scheme of white tiles in a kitchen, but could also be used in repeat.

DESIGN IDEA

TECHNIQUE

DIFFICULTY

see also kilns and firing **18–21** drying tiles **37** transferring motifs **53**

138 Circles and Squares

This is a simple tile to make, and is based on the balance of colors and shapes. Try different color combinations for variety.

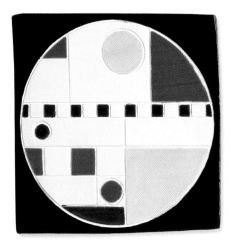

CLAY White earthenware fired to 2,012°F (1,100°C) biscuit and 1,868°F (1,020°C) glaze

Order of work

1 Prepare the tile and allow to dry to the leather-hard stage.

2 Transfer the design to the surface of the tile and sgraffito it in.

3 After biscuit firing, paint in the detail of the design using a selection of commercial paint-on glaze colors and fire to the recommended temperature.

You will need
- White earthenware clay
- Sgraffito tool
- Selection of commercial paint-on glazes
- Paintbrushes

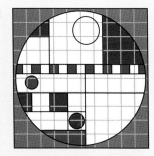

Arranging tiles
This tile should be positioned randomly in a scheme of plain tiles of similar colorways.

DESIGN IDEA

TECHNIQUE	DIFFICULTY

 1

see also kilns and firing **18–21** drying tiles **37** transferring motifs **53**

MOTIF

Rain

The watery look of this tile is enhanced by the use of reactive glaze, which gives an opalescent effect. Glazes of this type should be available from your ceramic supplier either in powder form or ready-mixed for use.

CLAY White stoneware fired to 1,832°F (1,000°C) biscuit and 2,300°F (1,260°C) glaze

Order of work

1 Prepare the tile and dry to leather hard.

2 Transfer the design to the surface of the tile and use a sgraffito and modeling tool to sgraffito and carve the detail.

3 After biscuit firing, paint over the tile with a selection of high-firing body stains.

4 Cover the tile with a coat of reactive or opalescent stoneware glaze and fire to the required temperature.

You will need

- Stoneware clay
- Sgraffito tool
- Modeling tool
- Selection of high-firing body stains
- Paintbrushes
- Stoneware glaze, reactive or opalescent

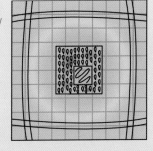

Arranging tiles

This tile would look good randomly mixed with other tiles made in a similar style.

DESIGN IDEA

TECHNIQUE

DIFFICULTY

see also kilns and firing **18–21** applying slip **32** drying tiles **37** oxide decoration **45–47** transferring motifs **53**

MOTIF

Seaweed
This is the only tile in the book that uses marbled slip as a base for decoration, because it can be quite wasteful of slip, which once mixed is unusable again. However, the effects can be exciting, so it is worth having a go.

CLAY White earthenware fired to 2,012°F (1,100°C) biscuit and 1,976°F (1,080°C) glaze

Order of work

1 Prepare the tile and allow it to dry to leather hard.

2 Marble the surface of the tile using two slip colors.

3 When the marbled surface has dried to the touch, paint a thick wash of black body stain over a nonabsorbent board. Allow the stain to dry.

4 Transfer the design to a sheet of paper, then place the paper over the board and redraw the pattern.

5 Lift the paper off the board and transfer the monoprint to the surface of the tile. After biscuit firing, apply a transparent glaze and fire to glaze temperature.

You will need
- White earthenware clay
- Two colored slips
- Black body stain
- Paintbrushes
- Paper and pencil
- Transparent earthenware glaze

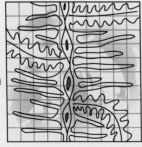

Arranging tiles
This tile would form a good random feature in a bathroom scheme of plain tiles.

DESIGN IDEA

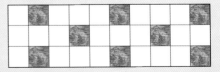

TECHNIQUE

DIFFICULTY

see also kilns and firing **18–21** marbling slip **35** drying tiles **37** transferring motifs **53**

MOTIF

Swirl

This tile has a very painterly look to it, and requires a freehand technique to achieve success, but other than that it is a simple motif to create.

CLAY Red earthenware fired to 2,012°F (1,100°C) biscuit and 1,976°F (1,080°C) glaze

Order of work

1 Apply a base coat of white slip to the surface of a leather-hard tile and allow to dry completely.

2 Transfer the design to the surface of the tile then paint in the detail using a selection of brush sizes and underglaze stains.

3 After biscuit firing, apply a coat of transparent glaze and fire to the necessary temperature.

You will need
- Red earthenware clay
- White slip
- Paintbrushes
- Selection of underglaze stains, including black
- Transparent earthenware glaze

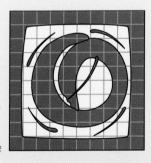

Arranging tiles

This tile would look good alternately repeated with plain tiles or others in a similar style.

DESIGN IDEA

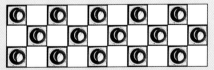

TECHNIQUE

DIFFICULTY

see also kilns and firing **18–21** drying tiles **37** underglaze painting **43** transferring motifs **53**

MOTIF

142 — Map

This tile was inspired by aerial views of towns and cities, and although now bearing little similarity to the original map, evidence of a street system is still vaguely evident.

CLAY White stoneware fired to 1,832°F (1,000°C) biscuit and 2,300°F (1,260°C) maturity

Order of work

1 Dampen a plaster bat and paint over the surface with a thick layer of white slip.

2 Roll a slab of clay over the slip on the bat then lift it off. The slip will only partially have stuck to the surface. Cut a tile from the slab.

3 Transfer the detail of the design to the surface of the tile. Roughly paint in the areas of colored slip then sgraffito the fine lines using a craft knife blade rather than a sgraffito tool.

4 After biscuit firing, paint a thin wash of manganese dioxide over the tile then wipe most of it back, so that it only remains in the detail. Fire the tile to 2,300°F (1,260°C) to vitrify the clay.

You will need
- Plaster bat
- Colored slips
- Paintbrushes
- White stoneware clay
- Rolling pin and roller guides
- Craft knife
- Manganese dioxide

Arranging tiles

This tile is designed as an artwork and would look good simply framed and hung on the wall.

DESIGN IDEA

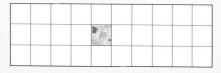

Abstract

TECHNIQUE

DIFFICULTY

see also kilns and firing **18–21** applying slip **32** drying tiles **37** oxide decoration **45–47** transferring motifs **53**

MOTIF

Hundertwasser: Windows

This colorful motif is based on window forms, each of which is contained in its own slip-trailed frame to give definition.

Order of work

1 Prepare the tile and allow to dry to the leather-hard stage.

2 Transfer the design to the surface of the tile and sgraffito the detail within each section or box of the motif.

3 Using black slip in a slip trailer, trail the outline of the frame.

4 After biscuit firing, paint in the detail of the windows with a selection of commercial paint-on glaze colors, then fire to the required temperature.

CLAY White earthenware fired to 2,012°F (1,100°C) biscuit and 1,868°F (1,020°C) glaze

You will need

- White earthenware clay
- Sgraffito tool
- Black slip
- Slip trailer
- Selection of commercial paint-on glazes
- Paintbrushes

Arranging tiles

This tile can be used randomly, as a feature in a scheme of plain tiles, or in repeat to form a very colorful display.

DESIGN IDEAS

TECHNIQUE

DIFFICULTY

see also kilns and firing **18–21** drying tiles **37** transferring motifs **53**

Hundertwasser: Psychedelic

Hundertwasser was an artist of the mid-twentieth century, whose work very much reflected the sentiments of the time, especially the colorful, psychedelic 1960s.

Order of work

1 Prepare the tile and dry to leather hard.

2 Transfer the outline of the design to the surface of the tile, then carefully paint in bands of underglaze color.

3 Using black slip, separate the bands of color with slip-trailed lines.

4 After biscuit firing, apply transparent glaze and fire to glaze temperature.

CLAY White earthenware fired to 2,012ºF (1,100ºC) biscuit and 1,976ºF (1,080ºC) glaze

You will need
- White earthenware clay
- Selection of underglaze stains
- Paintbrushes
- Black slip
- Slip trailer
- Transparent earthenware glaze

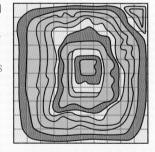

Arranging tiles
This tile could be used in repeat, for a very colorful effect, or as a feature in a scheme of plain tiles.

DESIGN IDEAS

TECHNIQUE

DIFFICULTY

see also kilns and firing **18–21** drying tiles **37** underglaze painting **43** transferring motifs **53**

MOTIF

Hundertwasser: Circles

Irregularly shaped circles feature widely in Hundertwasser's art, so it seemed appropriate to include them in this tile motif.

CLAY White earthenware fired to 2,012°F (1,100°C) biscuit and 1,976°F (1,080°C) glaze

Order of work

1 Carefully cut out the various sections of the circles using a selection of textured wallpapers.

2 Prepare a tile and transfer the outline of the design to its surface.

3 Position the wallpaper shapes in the outlined sections of the motif, textured side down, and roll them into the clay.

4 Remove the paper and paint the different areas of texture with a selection of underglaze stains.

5 After biscuit firing, apply transparent glaze and fire to the recommended temperature.

You will need

- Textured wallpapers
- White earthenware clay
- Rolling pin and roller guides
- Underglaze stains
- Paintbrushes
- Transparent earthenware glaze

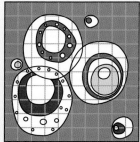

Arranging tiles

This tile is designed to form a feature in a scheme of plain tiles.

DESIGN IDEA

TECHNIQUE

DIFFICULTY

see also kilns and firing **18–21** drying tiles **37** underglaze painting **43** transferring motifs **53**

MOTIF

Hundertwasser: Minaret Crowns

The onion shapes of minaret crowns feature widely in Hundertwasser paintings and always very colorfully, so this tile has been painted in bright enamel colors to recreate that effect.

Order of work

1 Sponge an even coat of enamel color onto the surface of a glazed tile on the wall, and allow to dry.

2 Transfer the motif to the tile then paint in the detail using a selection of enamel colors.

3 Spray the surface of the tile with surface sealant to protect the decoration.

You will need
- Selection of on-glaze enamel colors
- Natural sponge
- Paintbrushes
- Surface sealant

Arranging tiles

This very colorful tile would quickly brighten up a scheme of dull plain tiles if randomly repeated in different colorways.

DESIGN IDEA

TECHNIQUE

DIFFICULTY

see also transferring motifs **53**

MOTIF

Klee: Color Grid

This linear design is typical of the work of Paul Klee, whose use of color was subtle and tonal. Textured wallpaper has been used to delineate some areas, in order to add visual interest to the motif.

Order of work

1 Cut out the textured wallpaper sections and use spray glue to fix them onto a cardboard tile template in the relevant position.

2 Roll the template over a slab of clay and cut the tile to size.

3 Remove the template and allow the tile to dry to the leather-hard stage, then transfer the rest of the design to the surface and sgraffito the lines.

4 After biscuit firing, paint the different sections using a selection of commercial paint-on glazes and fire to the required temperature.

CLAY White earthenware fired to 2,012°F (1,100°C) biscuit and 1,868°F (1,020°C) glaze

You will need

- Textured wallpaper
- Spray glue
- Cardboard
- White earthenware clay
- Rolling pin
- Sgraffito tool
- Paint-on glazes
- Paintbrushes

Arranging tiles

This motif could be used to good effect in a repeat format, or as a feature in an otherwise plain scheme of tiles.

DESIGN IDEAS

TECHNIQUE

DIFFICULTY

see also kilns and firing **18–21** drying tiles **37** transferring motifs **53**

Klee: Abstract Plant

I am not sure that this motif actually is a plant, but it has certain qualities that suggest it may be inspired by something organic, perhaps a thistle.

Order of work

1 Apply a base coat of slip color to a leather-hard tile.

2 Cut out the motif as a newspaper stencil and fix it to the surface of the tile with water.

3 Sponge several coats of a contrasting colored slip through the stencil, then remove the paper.

4 After biscuit firing, apply a coat of transparent glaze and fire to glaze temperature.

CLAY White earthenware fired to 2,012°F (1,100°C) biscuit and 1,976°F (1,080°C) glaze

You will need

- White earthenware clay
- Selection of colored slips
- Paintbrushes
- Newspaper
- Natural sponge
- Transparent earthenware glaze

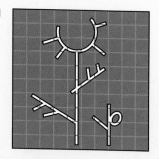

Arranging tiles

This tile would look especially effective if made in several different colorways, to be positioned randomly in an otherwise plain scheme.

DESIGN IDEA

TECHNIQUE

DIFFICULTY

1

see also kilns and firing **18–21** applying slip **32** drying tiles **37** transferring motifs **53**

MOTIF

Klee: Flowers and Water

This motif illustrates how art can inspire other disciplines, because it lends itself so well to interpretation in clay, but would also look good as a surface pattern for textiles.

CLAY White earthenware fired to 2,012°F (1,100°C) biscuit and 1,976°F (1,080°C) glaze

Order of work

1 Prepare the tile and allow to dry to the leather-hard stage.

2 Mask off the water sections of the tile with newspaper and sponge in the exposed areas with several coats of your first color of slip.

3 Remove the paper and mask off the areas already colored with more newspaper. Sponge the second slip color onto the clay, then remove the paper.

4 Transfer the detail of the motif to the surface of the tile and sgraffito it in.

5 After biscuit firing, apply a colored transparent glaze and fire to the necessary temperature.

You will need

- White earthenware clay
- Newspaper
- Colored slips
- Natural sponge
- Sgraffito tool
- Colored transparent earthenware glaze
- Paintbrush

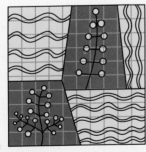

Arranging tiles

This tile would work best as a random feature in a scheme of plain tiles.

DESIGN IDEA

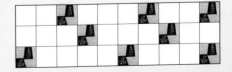

TECHNIQUE

DIFFICULTY

see also kilns and firing **18–21** drying tiles **37** transferring motifs **53**

Klee: Stenciled Plants These
very abstract shapes are perfect for the stenciling
technique, and are very easy to cut out.

Order of work

1 Lightly sponge a pale background color of
tile paint onto a glazed tile on the wall.
Allow to dry.

2 Transfer the design to stencil card and carefully
cut out the motif.

3 Spray a little repositioning glue on the back of
the stencil and secure it over the tile. Carefully
sponge or stipple a selection of tile paints over the
surface.

4 Remove the stencil and spray a covering layer
of sealant over the surface of the tile.

You will need

- Selection of tile paints
- Natural sponge
- Stencil card
- Craft knife
- Stencil brush (optional)
- Surface sealant
- Repositionable glue spray

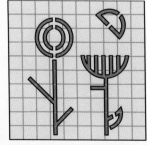

Arranging tiles

This tile could be used as a randomly repeated feature
to liven up a plain scheme of tiles, but would work
equally well in full repeat.

DESIGN IDEAS

TECHNIQUE

DIFFICULTY

see also transferring motifs **53**

MOTIF

Kandinsky: Hands

Kandinsky's art is very colorful, and lends itself well to interpretation as motifs for tiles.

CLAY Porcelain fired to 1,832°F (1,000°C) biscuit and 2,336°F (1,280°C) glaze. Luster firing to 1,346°F (730°C)

Order of work

1 Prepare the tile and allow it to dry to leather hard.

2 Transfer the design to the surface of the tile and carefully sgraffito the detail.

3 After biscuit firing, apply a transparent glaze and fire to glaze temperature.

4 Paint in the pattern detail with a selection of luster colors and precious metals, and fire again to the recommended temperature.

You will need
- Sgraffito tool
- Transparent stoneware glaze
- Selection of luster colors and precious metal luster
- Paintbrushes

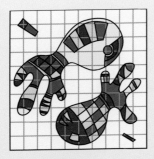

Arranging tiles
This motif would work best randomly positioned in a scheme of white tiles.

DESIGN IDEA

TECHNIQUE

DIFFICULTY

 1 **2** **3**

see also kilns and firing **18–21** drying tiles **37** transferring motifs **53**

MOTIF

Kandinsky: Abstract This motif incorporates two decorating techniques using subtle slip colors that are sharpened by black slip-trailed detail.

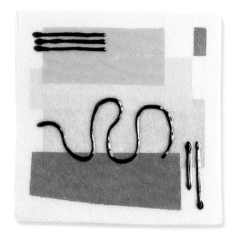

Order of work

1 Working on a leather-hard tile, sponge in the background slip colors using a separate newspaper stencil for each block shape. Dry each color off a little before applying the next one.

2 Carefully slip trail the lines using black slip.

3 After biscuit firing, apply a transparent glaze and fire to the recommended temperature.

CLAY White earthenware fired to 2,012°F (1,100°C) biscuit and 1,976°F (1,080°C) glaze

You will need
- White earthenware clay
- Colored slips
- Natural sponge
- Slip trailer
- Paintbrush
- Transparent glaze

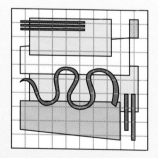

Arranging tiles
This tile looks most effective when randomly positioned in a scheme of plain tiles.

DESIGN IDEAS

TECHNIQUE

DIFFICULTY

see also kilns and firing **18–21** drying tiles **37** transferring motifs **53**

MOTIF

Kandinsky: Shapes The
composition of this tile appears mathematical, not only because of the shapes used, but in the balance and proportion of them within the square of the tile.

Order of work

1 Prepare the tile and dry to leather hard.

2 Transfer the design to the surface of the tile and sgraffito the outline.

3 After biscuit firing, cover the tile in black glaze, then wipe it back until it only remains in the detail. Glaze again, this time using a transparent glaze and fire to the required temperature.

4 Paint in the contained areas within the motif using a selection of luster colors, then refire to the necessary temperature.

CLAY Porcelain fired to 1,832°F (1,000°C) biscuit and 2,336°F (1,280°C) glaze. Luster firing to 1,346°F (730°C)

You will need

- Porcelain clay
- Sgraffito tool
- Black stoneware glaze
- Paintbrushes
- Transparent stoneware glaze
- Selection of luster colors

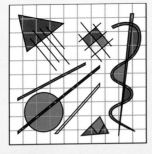

Arranging tiles

This tile would work as a random feature in a scheme of plain tiles, or could be used in repeat.

DESIGN IDEAS

TECHNIQUE

DIFFICULTY

see also kilns and firing **18–21** drying tiles **37** transferring motifs **53**

Modigliani: Figure

Modigliani painted the female figure in a stylized way, which has been simplified in this tile, yet still retains the signature qualities of the artist. Apply the surface color in a painterly way for good effect.

CLAY Red earthenware fired to 2,012°F (1,100°C) biscuit and 1,976°F (1,080°C) glaze

Order of work

1 Apply a thick coat of white slip to the surface of a leather-hard tile and allow it to dry out completely.

2 Transfer the outline of the design onto the surface of the tile then paint in the detail using a selection of underglaze stains.

3 After biscuit firing the tile, apply a transparent glaze and fire to glaze temperature.

You will need
- Red earthenware clay
- White slip
- Paintbrushes
- Selection of underglaze stains
- Transparent earthenware glaze

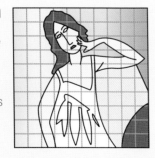

Arranging tiles

This tile is very much a one-off, which should be framed and hung as a work of art in its own right.

DESIGN IDEAS

TECHNIQUE

DIFFICULTY

 1 **2** **3**

see also kilns and firing **18–21** drying tiles **37** underglaze painting **43** transferring motifs **53**

MOTIF

Picasso: Profile
This tile looks very simple, but is actually quite complicated, because it includes all the slip decorating techniques, so it may be wise to practice them all for a better chance of success before you commit to the tile.

CLAY White earthenware fired to 2,012°F (1,100°C) biscuit and 1,976°F (1,080°C) glaze

Order of work

1 On a leather-hard tile, mask off the background areas with paper and use a natural sponge to fill the blocks of color with a selection of slips

2 Transfer the motif, including the face, onto the tile, then sgraffito in the detail.

3 Inlay the profile with another slip color, then use a metal kidney to scrape back the surplus slip when the surface has dried off sufficiently.

4 Carefully impress the circle shapes down the right side of the tile using the top of a pen or similar tool, and slip trail the remaining detail.

5 After biscuit firing, cover with transparent earthenware glaze and fire to glaze temperature.

You will need
- White earthenware clay
- Newspaper
- Colored slips
- Natural sponge
- Sgraffito tool
- Metal kidney
- Slip trailer
- Transparent earthenware glaze

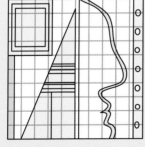

Arranging tiles
This tile is designed to form a random feature in a scheme of plain tiles, but would actually work as a border or column repeat.

DESIGN IDEAS

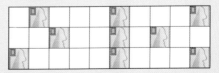

TECHNIQUE

DIFFICULTY

see also kilns and firing **18–21** drying tiles **37** transferring motifs **53**

Picasso: Face

Many of Picasso's paintings included abstracted parts of the face, and in this example the face appears to be secretly peering out from behind a screen or window.

CLAY Red earthenware fired to 2,012°F (1,100°C) biscuit and 1,976°F (1,080°C) glaze

Order of work

1 Prepare the tile and biscuit fire.

2 Transfer the design to the surface of the tile and carefully wax out the outline detail.

3 Cover the tile in white tin glaze, then paint in the color details using a selection of underglaze stains. Fire to glaze temperature.

You will need

- Red earthenware clay
- Wax emulsion
- Paintbrushes
- White tin glaze
- Selection of underglaze stains

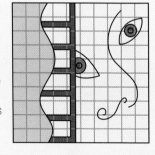

Arranging tiles

This tile is designed to form a feature in a scheme of plain tiles, but would also work as a quirky column repeat down the sides of a plain scheme.

DESIGN IDEAS

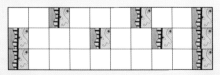

Libra, Gemini, Sagittarius, and Pisces

Use a different textured wallpaper and glaze colors for each sign.

For the Libra tile a red glaze was used.

Order of work

1 Transfer the design to some textured wallpaper and cut out the shapes.

2 Lay the shapes over a prepared tile, textured side down, and carefully roll them into the clay using roller guides to ensure the tile is kept even.

3 Before removing the paper, cut the tile back to shape using your template.

4 After biscuit firing, apply a colored transparent glaze that will pool in the texture, then fire to the required temperature.

You will need

- Textured wallpaper
- White earthenware clay
- Rolling pin and roller guides
- Selection of transparent earthenware glazes

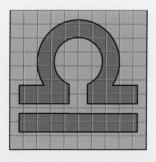

Arranging tiles

Use all of the zodiac tiles randomly within a wall of otherwise plain tiles.

DESIGN IDEA

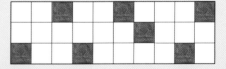

| TECHNIQUE | DIFFICULTY |

1

see also kilns and firing **18–21** drying tiles **37**

MOTIF

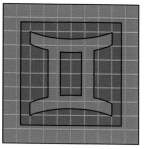

The Gemini tile uses a different wallpaper texture and a blue glaze has been used.

MOTIF

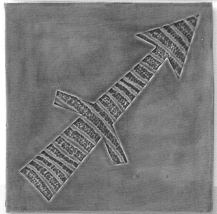

A green glaze has been used on the Sagittarius tile, and another variation on the textured wallpaper.

MOTIF

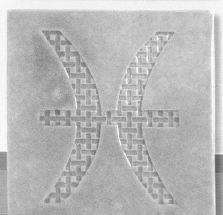

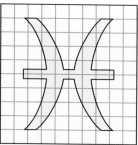

Orange glaze is the perfect choice for the Pisces tile, and variety can also be seen in the choice of textured wallpaper.

MOTIF

Leo, Virgo, Capricorn, and Scorpio

The following four zodiac signs all use the same technique, but different clays have been used to show the range of effects that can be achieved simply through firing to different temperatures.

Red earthenware clay and a black earthenware glaze have been used on the Leo tile.

Order of work

1 Prepare the tile and transfer the design to the surface.

2 Carefully carve out the design.

3 After biscuit firing, dip the tile in a glaze color of your choosing, then wipe back the glaze until it only remains in the carved-out detail. Fire to the recommended glaze temperature.

CLAYS Red earthenware fired to 2,012°F (1,100°C) biscuit and 1,976°F (1,080°C) glaze
Black earthenware fired to 1,832°F (1,000°C) biscuit and 1,832°F (1,000°C) glaze
Porcelain fired to 1,832°F (1,000°C) biscuit and 2,336°F (1,280°C) glaze

You will need
• Selection of clay types: for example, red earthenware, black earthenware, and porcelain
• Carving tools
• Selection of glazes to suit clay

Arranging tiles
Use all of the zodiac tiles randomly within a wall of otherwise plain tiles.

DESIGN IDEA

TECHNIQUE

DIFFICULTY

see also kilns and firing **18–21** drying tiles **37** transferring motifs **53**

MOTIF

For the Capricorn tile a red earthenware clay has been colored with a mid-brown earthenware glaze.

MOTIF

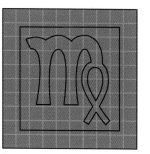

Black earthenware glaze is used over red earthenware clay for the Virgo tile.

MOTIF

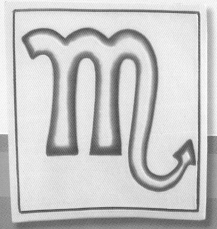

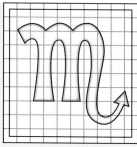

The Scorpio tile has been made from porcelain clay and covered with an orange glaze.

MOTIF

Cancer, Taurus, Aries, and Aquarius

The final four signs of the zodiac are made with paper resist and sgraffito. They use a similar color palette to fit a particular scheme, but you could vary this.

For the Cancer tile we used white earthenware clay and black and brown slip colors.

CLAY Red or white earthenware fired to 2,012°F (1,100°C) biscuit and 1,976°F (1,080°C) glaze

Order of work

1 Apply a base coat of slip color to a prepared tile and dry to leather hard.

2 Cut out a newspaper template of the zodiac motif, dampen it, and position it on the tile.

3 Sponge one or two contrasting slip colors over the tile, making sure not to totally obscure the base color—all layers of color should be seen. Using a natural sponge with an open texture will help.

4 Carefully remove the paper template and sgraffito any detail you want to add to the design.

5 After biscuit firing, cover with transparent glaze and fire to the appropriate temperature.

You will need

- Red or white earthenware clay
- Selection of colored slips
- Paintbrushes
- Newspaper
- Natural sponge
- Sgraffito tool
- Transparent earthenware glaze

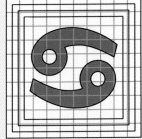

Arranging tiles

You can use all of the zodiac tiles randomly within a wall of otherwise plain tiles.

DESIGN IDEA

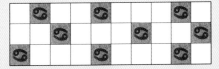

TECHNIQUE

DIFFICULTY

see also kilns and firing **18–21** mixing colors for slip **31** drying tiles **37** transferring motifs **53**

MOTIF

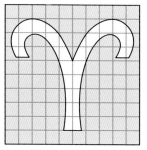

The Taurus tile uses red earthenware clay and brown and orange slip colors.

MOTIF

Tan and orange slip colors have been used on white earthenware clay for the Aries tile, and variety can also be seen in the sgraffito detail.

MOTIF

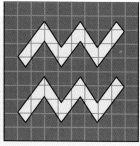

For the Aquarius tile a sienna slip has been used as a base coat, with cream sponging. Notice that the sgraffito detail has also been varied.

MOTIF

Circle Knot

This pattern uses four interlocking circles as a starting point for the rest of the design, and is quite complex to complete, therefore you will need to transfer the design to the tile very accurately to ensure successful results.

CLAY Red earthenware fired to 2,012°F (1,100°C) biscuit and 1,976°F (1,080°C) glaze

Order of work

1 Prepare the tile and dry to leather hard.

2 Transfer the design to the surface of the tile and sgraffito the outline quite deeply to give good definition to the design.

3 After biscuit firing, cover the tile with a coat of colored glaze and wipe it back so that it only remains in the detail of the motif. Fire the tile to glaze temperature.

You will need
- Red earthenware clay
- Sgraffito tool
- Colored earthenware glaze
- Paintbrush

Arranging tiles
This tile could form a complete repeat or be used as a random feature in an otherwise plain scheme of tiles.

DESIGN IDEAS

TECHNIQUE

DIFFICULTY

Linocut Knotwork Design

You will need a fine lino-cutting tool for this design and some patience, because the motif is quite complicated and demands care to cut out.

MOTIF

CLAY White stoneware fired to 1,832°F (1,000°C) biscuit and 2,300°F (1,260°C) glaze

Order of work

1 Transfer the design to a lino block and carefully cut it out.

2 Prepare the tile and roll the lino block into it to transfer the design. Lift the block carefully off the clay then cut the tile back to shape.

3 After biscuit firing, apply a wash of copper carbonate to the surface of the tile, then cover with a reactive or opaque glaze and fire to the recommended temperature.

You will need
- 6-in. (15-cm) square lino block
- Lino-cutting tool
- White stoneware clay
- Rolling pin
- Copper carbonate
- Paintbrushes
- Stoneware glaze

Arranging tiles

This tile will work equally well as a complete repeat or as a random feature in a plain scheme of tiles.

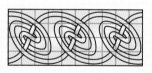

DESIGN IDEAS

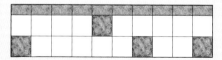

TECHNIQUE

DIFFICULTY

see also kilns and firing **18–21** Drying tiles **37** underglaze painting **43** transferring motifs **53**

MOTIF

Zoomorphic Motif with Knot

This stylized animal forms a typical Celtic knot motif, incorporating a border at top and bottom. Use as a border repeat, with the creatures chasing one another across the wall.

CLAY Red earthenware fired to 2,012ºF (1,100ºC) biscuit and 1,976ºF (1,080ºC) glaze

Order of work

1 Prepare the tile and allow to dry to the leather-hard stage.

2 Transfer the design to the surface of the tile and carefully sgraffito the outline of the motif.

3 After biscuit firing, paint an oxide wash over the surface of the tile then cover with white tin glaze and fire to glaze temperature.

You will need
- Red earthenware clay
- Sgraffito tool
- Copper oxide
- Paintbrushes
- White tin glaze

Arranging tiles

This tile is meant to form a border repeat, or be used as a line repeat in a plain scheme.

DESIGN IDEA

TECHNIQUE

DIFFICULTY

see also kilns and firing **18–21** drying tiles **37** oxide decoration **45–47** transferring motifs **53**

Key Pattern

This typical key pattern is much simpler to create than many other Celtic motifs, and forms a wonderful repeat that could be used in any number of locations within the home.

CLAY Black earthenware fired to 1,940°F (1,060°C) biscuit only

Order of work

1 Prepare the tile and allow it to dry to leather hard.

2 Transfer the design to the surface of the tile and carefully sgraffito the outline of the motif.

3 Paint over the motif with white slip and, when sufficiently dry to work with, use a metal kidney to scrape away the excess slip and reveal the pattern lines.

4 When dry, fire to the recommended biscuit temperature.

You will need

- Black earthenware clay
- Sgraffito tool
- White slip
- Paintbrush
- Metal kidney

Arranging tiles
This tile forms a complete repeat.

DESIGN IDEAS

TECHNIQUE

DIFFICULTY

see also kilns and firing **18–21** drying tiles **37** transferring motifs **53**

MOTIF

Knot Cross
This knotwork motif is simple enough to carve out in low relief to make a plaster mold for quick, multiple-batch production.

CLAY White earthenware fired to 2,012°F (1,100°C) biscuit and 1,976°F (1,080°C) glaze

Order of work

1 Prepare a plain tile and dry to leather hard.

2 Transfer the design to the surface of the tile and carve the outline to form a low relief.

3 Cast the model in plaster, then, when the mold is dry, make the tile by press molding.

4 After biscuit firing, glaze the tile using a colored transparent glaze, allowing it to pool in the detail for definition, or sponge another transparent glaze over the first for special effect.

You will need
- White earthenware clay
- Modeling tool
- Potter's plaster
- Colored transparent earthenware glazes
- Natural sponge or stencil brush

Arranging tiles
This tile can be used to form a complete repeat.

DESIGN IDEA

TECHNIQUE

DIFFICULTY

see also kilns and firing **18–21** mold making **22** drying tiles **37** transferring motifs **53**

175

Stencil Knot
This is a simple but effective knot motif that can be used to decorate a wall of plain tiles. Use it either in repeat, as a border, or randomly.

Order of work

1 Transfer the design to a sheet of stencil card that is the same size as your tile and carefully cut out the motif.

2 Spray a little repositioning glue on the back of the stencil and secure it over the tile on the wall. Apply the tile paints following any of the stenciling methods.

3 Remove the stencil and seal the surface of the tile.

You will need

- Stencil card and a sharp craft knife
- Repositioning spray glue
- Selection of tile paints
- Natural sponge or stencil brush
- Surface sealant

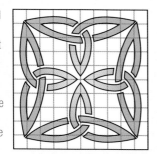

Arranging tiles

This design can form a complete repeat, a border repeat, or be used as a random feature in a scheme of plain tiles.

DESIGN IDEAS

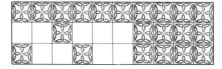

TECHNIQUE

DIFFICULTY

see also transferring motifs **53**

MOTIF

Key Pattern No. 2 This motif
combines two decorating techniques and demands
a little patience to make accurately, even though it looks simple.

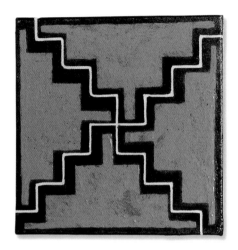

CLAY Black earthenware fired to 1,940°F (1,060°C)
biscuit and 1,868°F (1,020°C) glaze

Order of work

1 Prepare the tile and dry to leather hard.

2 Transfer the central stepped cross lines to the surface of the tile and sgraffito the lines.

3 Fill in the lines with white slip and, when sufficiently dry to work with, use a metal kidney to scrape away excess slip and reveal the pattern.

4 Cut out a newspaper template to cover the inlayed lines and frame of the tile, dampen it, and position it on the tile. Sponge in the pattern with colored slip.

5 After biscuit firing, paint over the tile with a transparent glaze and fire to the required temperature.

You will need
- Black earthenware clay
- Sgraffito tool
- Colored slips
- Paintbrushes
- Metal kidney
- Newspaper
- Natural sponge
- Transparent earthenware glaze

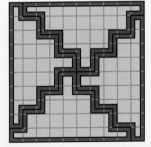

Arranging tiles
This tile can be used randomly or in repeat.

DESIGN IDEAS

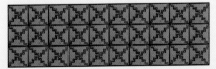

TECHNIQUE

DIFFICULTY

see also kilns and firing **18–21** applying slip **32** drying tiles **37** transferring motifs **53**

MOTIF

Key Pattern Border

This border is designed to work with the Key Pattern opposite, though it would also work as a border to a wall of plain tiles in a complementary color.

CLAY Black earthenware fired to 1,940°F (1,060°C) biscuit and 1,868°F (1,020°C) glaze

Order of work

1 Prepare the tile and dry to leather hard.

2 Cut out a newspaper stencil of the motif, dampen it, and fix it to the surface of the tile.

3 Carefully sponge colored slips over the entire surface of the tile, including the paper shape.

4 After biscuit firing, apply transparent earthenware glaze and fire to the required temperature.

You will need
- Black earthenware clay
- Newspaper
- Selection of colored slips
- Natural sponge
- Transparent earthenware glaze
- Paintbrush

Arranging tiles

This tile is designed to border another design of tiles, but could also border a plain scheme in the same color.

DESIGN IDEA

TECHNIQUE

DIFFICULTY

see also kilns and firing **18–21** applying slip **32** drying tiles **37** transferring motifs **53**

MOTIF

1950s Low Relief The design
for this molded tile is inspired by 1950s' textiles,
and forms a complete repeat on all sides. Once you have made
the mold you can either slip cast the tiles or press mold them.

Order of work

1 Make the mold for the tile and either slip cast or press mold the clay to make the tile.

2 Cover the tile with a colored transparent glaze, which will pool in the detail, and fire to glaze temperature.

CLAY White earthenware fired to 2,012°F (1,100°C) biscuit and 1,976°F (1,080°C) glaze

You will need
- Potter's plaster
- White earthenware clay
- Colored transparent earthenware glaze
- Paintbrush

Arranging tiles
This tile forms a perfect repeat on all four sides

DESIGN IDEA

TECHNIQUE

DIFFICULTY

see also kilns and firing **18–21** mold making **22** drying tiles **37** transferring motifs **53**

1950s Still Life
This design is typical of the sort found decorating the surfaces of ceramics and textiles in the 1950s, depicting a stylized but lively drawing of a bowl of fruit.

Order of work

1 Paint the surface of a leather-hard tile with a painterly wash of two or three slip colors.

2 When the slip is touch dry, transfer the design to the surface of the tile and sgraffito the detail, so that the clay body shows through the lines.

3 After biscuit firing, apply a transparent glaze and fire to the required temperature.

CLAY Red earthenware fired to 2,012°F (1,100°C) biscuit and 1,976°F (1,080°C) glaze

You will need
• Red earthenware clay
• Selection of colored slips
• Paintbrushes
• Sgraffito tool
• Transparent earthenware glaze

Arranging tiles
This tile would look great randomly placed with other tiles in the same style, especially in a kitchen.

DESIGN IDEA

TECHNIQUE

DIFFICULTY

1 **2**

see also kilns and firing **18–21** applying slip **32** drying tiles **37** Transferring motifs **53**

MOTIF

1950s Surface Pattern The
inspiration for this tile was taken from a dinnerware pattern. The design looks great in repeat, and could make a stunning decoration feature for a wall almost anywhere in the home.

CLAY White earthenware fired to 2,012°F (1,100°C) biscuit and 1,976°F (1,080°C) glaze

Order of work

1 On a leather-hard tile, mask off the four areas next to the central square with damp newspaper, then sponge three coats of colored slip on the exposed areas. Remove the paper.

2 Mask off the corner sections, the center, and two opposite sections with more newspaper and sponge a second slip color over the remaining two unmasked sections of the tile. Remove the paper.

3 In the areas shown, sponge over three of the squares with a contrasting colored slip.

4 Wash a black body stain over a nonabsorbent board and let dry. Place a sheet of paper with the pattern on over the top and redraw. Transfer the monoprint on the paper to the tile before biscuit firing. Cover with transparent glaze and fire.

You will need
• White earthenware clay
• Newspaper
• Colored slips
• Natural sponges
• Black body stain
• Paper and pencil
• Transparent earthenware glaze
• Paintbrush

Arranging tiles
This tile would repeat to form a great feature wall in any number of rooms.

DESIGN IDEAS

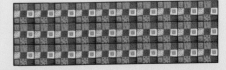

TECHNIQUE

DIFFICULTY

 1 **2** **3**

see also kilns and firing **18–21** drying tiles **37** transferring motifs **53**

1950s Abstract
This design is inspired by block-printed textiles. Only the outline of the original design has been used and reassembled to form this inlaid tile.

Order of work

1 Prepare the tile and dry to leather hard.

2 Transfer the design to the surface of the tile and sgraffito the outline of the design.

3 Fill in the lines with colored slips, and when the slips are dry enough scrape them back, using a metal kidney, to reveal the pattern below.

4 After biscuit firing, apply transparent glaze and fire to glaze temperature.

CLAY Black earthenware fired to 2,012ºF (1,100ºC) biscuit and 1,976ºF (1,080ºC) glaze

You will need
- Black earthenware clay
- Sgraffito tool
- Selection of colored slips
- Paintbrushes
- Metal kidney
- Transparent earthenware glaze

Arranging tiles
This tile forms a good repeat, but would also look effective as a random feature in a scheme of plain tiles in the same clay type.

DESIGN IDEAS

TECHNIQUE

DIFFICULTY

see also kilns and firing **18–21** drying tiles **37** transferring motifs **53**

1960s Flower

There had to be a flower in the 1960s section of the retro category, given that it was the time of "flower power," and this tile is a great example of how commercially glazed tiles can be refired to good effect.

Order of work

1 Transfer the outline of the design to a ready-glazed commercial tile.

2 Paint in the various colors using commercial paint-on glazes, allowing each color to dry before applying the next, to avoid one color bleeding into another.

3 Fire to the recommended glaze temperature.

NOTE The glazes used in this example were designed to fire at 1,868°F (1,020°C) maturity, so this tile was an experiment that worked very well, given that the tile was fired to 1,976°F (1,080°C).

You will need
- Ready-glazed commercial tile
- Selection of commercial paint-on glazes
- Paintbrushes

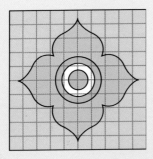

Arranging tiles
This tile forms a fantastic repeat that could be used in any number of locations in the home.

DESIGN IDEA

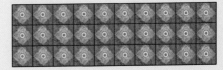

TECHNIQUE

DIFFICULTY

see also kilns and firing **18–21** transferring motifs **53**

MOTIF

  183

1960s Hearts

A potent symbol of the 1960s was the heart, which represented the idea of free love. The ideals seem naive and dated now, but the imagery is going through something of a revival.

CLAY White earthenware fired to 2,012°F (1,100°C) biscuit and 1,868°F (1,020°C) glaze

Order of work

1 Transfer the design to the surface of a biscuit-fired tile.

2 Paint on one color of commercial paint-on glaze at a time, allowing each one to dry thoroughly before painting on the next, to avoid the colors bleeding into one another.

3 Fire to the recommended glaze temperature.

You will need
- White earthenware clay
- Selection of commercial paint-on glazes
- Paintbrushes

Arranging tiles
This tile forms a complete repeat that would make a great feature wall.

DESIGN IDEA

TECHNIQUE

DIFFICULTY

 1 **2**

see also kilns and firing **18–21** drying tiles **37** transferring motifs **53**

MOTIF

184 1960s Lines and Circles

This motif is taken directly from a 1960s' textile pattern, but has a totally contemporary look that would easily fit into any modern interior.

CLAY White stoneware fired to 1,832°F (1,000°C) biscuit and 2,300°F (1,260°C) glaze

Order of work

1 Prepare the tile and dry to leather hard.

2 Transfer the design to the surface of the tile and sgraffito the lines of the motif.

3 After biscuit firing, apply a coat of black glaze and wipe it back until it only remains in the lines. Fire the tile to glaze temperature.

You will need

- White stoneware clay
- Black stoneware glaze
- Paintbrush
- Sgraffito tool

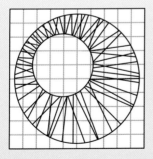

Arranging tiles

This tile could be placed randomly in a scheme of plain tiles, or be used in repeat to cover a whole wall.

DESIGN IDEAS

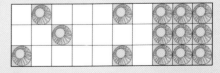

TECHNIQUE

DIFFICULTY

1

see also kilns and firing **18–21** drying tiles **37** transferring motifs **53**

1960s Psychedelic with Border

Wavy psychedelic patterns were very popular in the 1960s, and, of all the designs to come out of that decade, seem the most dated now, but they still have a certain nostalgic appeal.

CLAY Red earthenware fired to 2,012°F (1,100°C) biscuit and 1,976°F (1,080°C) glaze

Order of work

1 Cover the surface of a leather-hard tile with a base coat of white slip and allow to dry completely.

2 Transfer the outline of the design to the surface of the tile, then paint in the various colors with a selection of underglaze stains.

3 After biscuit firing, cover with transparent glaze and fire to the necessary temperature.

MOTIF

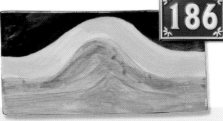

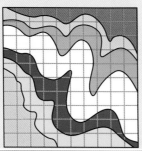

You will need
- Red earthenware clay
- White slip
- Paintbrushes
- Selection of underglaze stains
- Transparent earthenware glaze

Arranging tiles
This tile can be used in repeat with the border, or as a random tile in a plain scheme.

DESIGN IDEAS

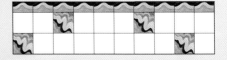

TECHNIQUE

DIFFICULTY

 1

see also kilns and firing **18–21** drying tiles **37** underglaze painting **43** transferring motifs **53**

MOTIF

1970s Trees
This style of decoration was very popular in the brown glaze, studio ceramic period of the early 1970s, when Bernard Leach-style pots sold like hot cakes.

CLAY Red earthenware fired to 2,012°F (1,100°C) biscuit and 1,976°F (1,080°C) glaze

Order of work

1 Transfer the design to the surface of a biscuit-fired tile.

2 Wax out the branches of the trees on either side of the central tree, then paint over the tile with a wash of manganese dioxide.

3 Wax out the tree trunks and branches of the central tree, cover the whole tile in white tin glaze—it will not stick to the waxed areas—and fire to glaze temperature.

You will need

- Red earthenware clay
- Wax emulsion
- Paintbrushes
- Manganese dioxide
- White tin glaze

Arranging tiles

This tile looks effective when randomly positioned in a scheme of tiles in similar colors, or it could be used as a border repeat.

DESIGN IDEA

TECHNIQUE

DIFFICULTY

1 **2**

see also kilns and firing **18–21** drying tiles **37** oxide decoration **45–47** wax resist **46** transferring motifs **53**

MOTIF

1970s Surface Pattern This
surface pattern was adapted from a textile design
from the early 1970s, and is painted in enamel colors onto a
commercially glazed tile.

Order of work

1 Transfer the design to the surface of a glazed tile.

2 Paint in the enamel colors one at a time, allowing each to dry before applying the next, to prevent the colors bleeding into one another.

3 Spray over the tile with surface sealant.

You will need
• Ready-glazed tile
• Selection of on-glaze enamel colors
• Paintbrushes
• Surface sealant

Arranging tiles
This tile would make a great repeat pattern, using different but complementary colorways.

DESIGN IDEA

TECHNIQUE

DIFFICULTY

1

see also transferring motifs **53**

1970s Flower A simple glaze-on-glaze
technique was used to create this motif, which
could be made in any number of colorways for a fantastic effect.

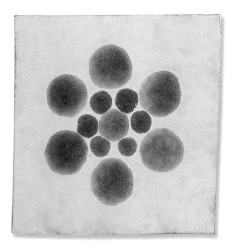

CLAY Red earthenware fired to 2,012°F (1,100°C)
biscuit and 1,976°F (1,080°C) glaze

Order of work

1 Apply a base coat of white tin glaze to the
surface of a biscuit-fired tile.

2 Transfer the design to the glazed surface and
paint in the circles of the design with two or
three different colored earthenware glazes, then
fire to glaze temperature.

You will need
- Red
earthenware clay
- White tin glaze
- Paintbrushes
- Selection of
earthenware
glazes

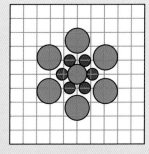

Arranging tiles
This tile could be placed randomly in a scheme of
plain tiles, but would work just as well in repeat if
made in different colorways.

DESIGN IDEAS

TECHNIQUE

DIFFICULTY

see also kilns and firing **18–21** drying tiles **37** transferring motifs **53**

1970s Corner Pattern
Typical of the sharp design lines that emerged in the 1970s, in contrast to the flowing trends of the 1960s, this tile is carved in low relief and makes a wonderful repeat in fours or as a border.

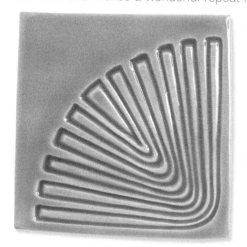

Order of work

1 Prepare the tile and allow to dry to the leather-hard stage.

2 Transfer the design to the surface of the tile and carefully carve out the detail.

3 After biscuit firing, apply a colored transparent glaze, allowing it to pool in the detail, and fire to glaze temperature.

CLAY White earthenware fired to 2,012°F (1,100°C) biscuit and 1,976°F (1,080°C) glaze

You will need
- White earthenware clay
- Modeling tool
- Colored transparent earthenware glaze
- Paintbrush

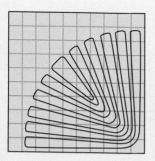

Arranging tiles
This tile looks great in repeats of four, but also makes a good border repeat to fit a scheme of plain tiles.

DESIGN IDEA

TECHNIQUE

DIFFICULTY

see also kilns and firing **18–21** drying tiles **37** transferring motifs **53**

MOTIF

Hexagonal Snowflake This
simple snowflake motif is the perfect fit for this
hexagonal tile, which could be used as a floor tile if left unglazed.

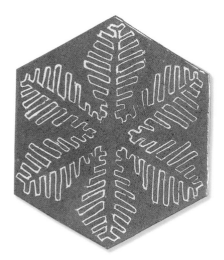

CLAY Red earthenware fired to 2,012°F (1,100°C)
biscuit and 1,976°F (1,080°C) glaze

Order of work

1 Prepare the tile and allow to dry to the leather-hard stage.

2 Transfer the design to the surface of the tile and sgraffito the outline of the snowflake.

3 Paint over the lines with a white or colored slip. When the slip has dried sufficiently, use a metal kidney to scrape away the surplus to reveal the pattern underneath.

4 After biscuit firing, apply transparent glaze and fire to glaze temperature.

You will need
- Red earthenware clay
- Sgraffito tool
- White or colored slip
- Paintbrush
- Metal kidney
- Transparent earthenware glaze

Arranging tiles
This tile forms a complete repeat.

DESIGN IDEA

TECHNIQUE

DIFFICULTY

see also kilns and firing **18–21** drying tiles **37** transferring motifs **53**

192 Hexagonal Star

This tile looks very different from the previous one (opposite), but is actually made the same way. It is simply made in a different clay and inlayed with black slip.

CLAY White earthenware fired to 2,012°F (1,100°C) biscuit and 1,976°F (1,080°C) glaze

Order of work

1 Prepare the tile and dry to leather hard.

2 Transfer the design to the surface of the tile and sgraffito the outline of the star.

3 Paint over the lines with black slip. When the slip has dried sufficiently, use a metal kidney to scrape away the surplus to reveal the pattern underneath.

4 After biscuit firing, apply colored transparent glaze and fire to glaze temperature.

You will need

- White earthenware clay
- Sgraffito tool
- Black slip
- Paintbrushes
- Metal kidney
- Colored transparent earthenware glaze

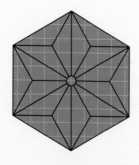

Arranging tiles

This tile forms a complete repeat.

DESIGN IDEA

MOTIF

Hexagonal Bolt
This tile is so named because the motif is reminiscent of the ends of bolts. It is designed to mix and match with the two previous hexagonal tiles, all of which can be made in the same colorways if preferred.

Order of work

1 Prepare the tile and allow to dry to the leather-hard stage.

2 Cut out the bolt shapes from newspaper, dampen them, and fix them in position onto the surface of the tile. Sponge over the tile using a selection of colored slips, then carefully remove the paper stencils.

3 After biscuit firing, apply a colored transparent glaze and fire to the recommended temperature.

CLAY White earthenware fired to 2,012°F (1,100°C) biscuit and 1,976°F (1,080°C) glaze

You will need
• Selection of colored slips
• Natural sponge
• Colored transparent earthenware glaze
• Paintbrush
• Newspaper

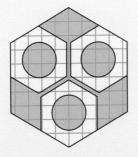

Arranging tiles
This tile forms a complete repeat.

DESIGN IDEA

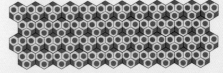

TECHNIQUE

DIFFICULTY

see also kilns and firing **18–21** drying tiles **37** transferring motifs **53**

Hexagonal Knot This is a simple
adaptation of the previous one, in that the bolt design is broken up so that it is interlocking in the style of a Celtic knot. It is a good example of how designs can be reworked to look very different.

Order of work

1 Prepare the tile and dry to leather hard.

2 Transfer the design to the surface of the tile and sgraffito the motif.

3 After biscuit firing, apply a colored transparent glaze and fire to the necessary temperature.

CLAY Red earthenware fired to 2,012°F (1,100°C) biscuit and 1,976°F (1,080°C) glaze

You will need
• Red earthenware clay
• Sgraffito tool
• Colored transparent earthenware glaze
• Paintbrush

Arranging tiles
This tile forms a complete repeat.

DESIGN IDEA

TECHNIQUE

DIFFICULTY

1 2

see also kilns and firing **18–21** drying tiles **37** transferring motifs **53**

MOTIF

Geometric Lino Relief

This design is easy to cut from a lino block, and the raised outline that results when the tile is made creates a perfect division of sections for commercial paint-on glazes.

CLAY White earthenware fired to 2,012°F (1,100°C) biscuit and 1,976°F (1,080°C) glaze

Order of work

1 Transfer the design to a lino block and carefully cut it out using a range of cutting tools to create different lines and textures.

2 Roll the lino block onto a slab of clay, lift the block off the clay carefully, then cut the tile to the correct shape.

3 After biscuit firing, paint the sections of the tile using a selection of commercial paint-on glaze colors, and fire to the required temperature.

You will need

- 6-in. (15-cm) square lino block
- Lino-cutting tools
- White earthenware clay
- Rolling pin and roller guides
- Selection of commercial glazes
- Paintbrushes

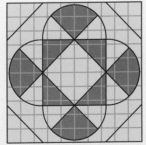

Arranging tiles

This tile forms a complete repeat, but could also be used as a feature in a scheme of plain tiles, or as a border.

DESIGN IDEA

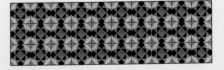

TECHNIQUE

DIFFICULTY

see also kilns and firing **18–21** drying tiles **37** transferring motifs **53**

MOTIF

Curvate Geometric

This tile combines the techniques of paper resist and sgraffito, and although it looks very simple, it actually requires some skill to complete successfully, because of the arrangement of the stencil.

CLAY Red earthenware fired to 2,012°F (1,100°C) biscuit and 1,976°F (1,080°C) glaze

Order of work

1 Prepare the tile and let it dry to leather hard.

2 Cut newspaper to size, and mark out the design. Use a craft knife to cut out the inner circle and the outer rotating sections. Keep the cutout sections.

3 Use water to fix the stencil onto the tile surface, then sponge on two or three coats of colored slip. When the slip is touch dry, remove the paper.

4 Fix the cutouts over the parts of the motif already covered with slip, and sponge a second slip color over the inner section. Let dry and remove the paper.

5 Sgraffito the lines radiating from the inner circle, then, after biscuit firing, cover with transparent glaze and fire to glaze temperature.

You will need

- Red earthenware clay
- Newspaper
- Craft knife
- Selection of colored slips
- Natural sponge
- Sgraffito tool
- Transparent earthenware glaze

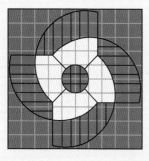

Arranging tiles

This tile forms a complete repeat.

DESIGN IDEA

Geometric Block
This motif is simply created by dividing squares in half diagonally, then dividing one half again in the same way. The division could go on almost endlessly, but this is a good starting point for further experimentation.

CLAY White earthenware fired to 2,012°F (1,100°C) biscuit and 1,868°F (1,020°C) glaze

Order of work

1 Prepare the tile and leave until it is almost dry.

2 Transfer the design to the surface of the tile. Using a selection of underglaze stains, paint in the various sections, applying all of one color at a time.

3 After biscuit firing, apply transparent glaze and fire to the recommended temperature.

You will need
- White earthenware clay
- Selection of underglaze stains
- Paintbrushes
- Transparent earthenware glaze

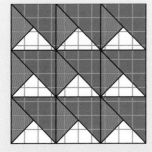

Arranging tiles
This tile forms a complete repeat.

DESIGN IDEA

TECHNIQUE

DIFFICULTY

see also kilns and firing **18–21** drying tiles **37** underglaze painting **43** transferring motifs **53**

MOTIF

Curvate Fans

The template for this tile takes time to make, because each curvate section has to be cut out in two parts from different wallpapers, then reassembled and stuck together. However, the template can be re-used many times.

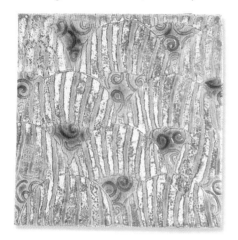

CLAY White stoneware fired to 1,832°F (1,000°C) biscuit and 2,300°F (1,260°C) glaze

Order of work

1 Transfer the complete design to the back of a sheet of textured wallpaper, then cut out the sections as drawn.

2 Repeat Step 1 with a different textured wallpaper, then, using adhesive tape, carefully join the upper parts of section one to the lower parts of section two. Now reassemble all the sections using adhesive tape on the back, to hold it all together.

3 Roll the template into a slab of clay, then cut the tile to size.

4 After biscuit firing, paint body stains and oxides over the pattern to delineate the sections, then cover with a reactive or opaque glaze and fire to the required temperature.

You will need

- Textured wallpaper
- White stoneware clay
- Rolling pin
- Body stains and oxides
- Paintbrushes
- Stoneware glaze

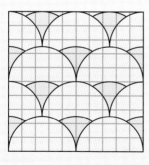

Arranging tiles

This tile forms a complete repeat.

DESIGN IDEA

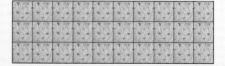

MOTIF

199

Diamonds and Circles This

simple motif is designed by the division of squares, but introduces a circle to visually enliven the pattern.

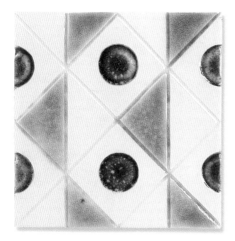

CLAY White earthenware fired to 2,012°F (1,100°C) biscuit and 1,868°F (1,020°C) glaze

Order of work

1 Prepare the tile and dry to leather hard.

2 Transfer the design to the surface of the tile then carefully carve out the motif using a modeling or similar tool.

3 After biscuit firing, first cover the whole tile in transparent glaze, then carefully paint over the individual sections with other colored transparent glazes. Fire the tile to glaze temperature.

You will need

- White earthenware clay
- Modeling tool
- Transparent earthenware glaze
- Colored transparent earthenware glazes
- Paintbrushes

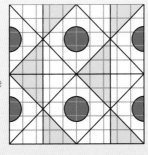

Arranging tiles

This tile forms a complete repeat.

DESIGN IDEA

TECHNIQUE	DIFFICULTY

see also kilns and firing **18–21** drying tiles **37** transferring motifs **53**

MOTIF

200 Geometric Paper Cut

The hardest part of making this tile is cutting out the paper stencil, but even this is more time-consuming than difficult. You could simplify the design by leaving certain areas uncut if you feel it is too much.

CLAY Red earthenware fired to 2,012°F (1,100°C) biscuit and 1,976°F (1,080°C) glaze

Order of work

1 Apply a base coat of white slip to the surface of a leather-hard tile and allow to dry completely.

2 Cut out the paper stencil, dampen it, and position it over the tile. Paint over the stencil with black underglaze stain. The stain may bleed under the stencil a little but this adds to the finish in this case.

3 After biscuit firing, apply transparent glaze and fire to glaze temperature.

You will need

- Red earthenware clay
- White slip
- Paintbrushes
- Newspaper
- Black underglaze stain
- Transparent earthenware glaze

Arranging tiles

This tile forms a complete repeat.

DESIGN IDEA

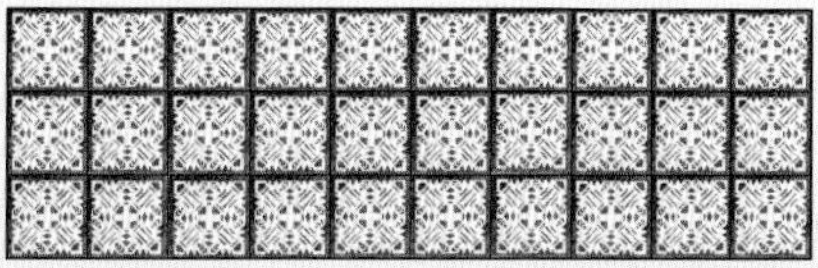

TECHNIQUE

DIFFICULTY

1

see also kilns and firing **18–21** applying slip **32** drying tiles **37** underglaze painting **43** transferring motifs **53**

Glossary

Alumina One of the three main components of glaze, having a very high melting point. Usually added to a glaze in the form of powdered clay. Hydrated alumina is also used as a constituent of bat wash.

Ball clay A fine, plastic clay, usually white or off-white firing. So named because of the method of transporting the clay in round lumps.

Bat A plaster or wooden disk for moving tiles without handling, or for drying clay.

Bat wash A mixture of alumina and china clay used as a protective coating for kiln shelves.

Biscuit Clay ware after the first firing, usually around 1,830°F (1,000°C).

Biscuit firing The first firing of pottery to mature the clay and make it permanent. For biscuit firing, tiles may be stacked inside or on top of one another because there is no glaze to stick them together.

Body The term used to describe a particular mixture of clay, such as stoneware, or earthenware body.

Casting Making tiles by pouring liquid clay into a plaster mold.

Casting slip A liquid slip used in the process of making objects using plaster molds.

Ceramic Any clay form that is fired in a kiln.

China clay A pure-white-burning, nonplastic body clay, usually used in combination with other clays or in glazes.

Cottle The wall used to surround a shape to be cast in plaster.

Crank A refractory support for firing tiles.

Delftware A type of Majolica developed in the Netherlands and named after the town in which the tiles were made.

Dipping Applying a slip or glaze by immersion.

Earthenware Pottery fired to a relatively low temperature. The body remains porous and usually requires glazing if it is to be used for domestic ware.

Elements The metal heating coils in an electric kiln.

Enamels Low-firing commercially manufactured colors that are painted onto a fired surface and re-fired to melt them into the glaze.

Encaustic Another (old) name for inlay where designs pressed into clay are filled with a contrasting clay color.

Firing The process by which ceramic ware is heated in a kiln to harden or glaze it.

Firing chamber The interior of a kiln in which pottery is fired.

Firing cycle The gradual raising and lowering of the temperature of a kiln to fire ceramics.

Glaze A thin glassy layer on the surface of ceramics.

Glaze stain Commercially manufactured colorant that is added to glaze.

Greenware Unfired clay ware.

Grog Fired clay that is ground into particles, ranging from a fine dust to coarse sand. Added to soft clay it adds strength, resists warping, and helps reduce thermal shock.

Incising The process of carving or cutting a design into a raw clay surface.

Kidney A kidney-shaped scraper, made in metal, plastic, or wood.

Kiln A device in which pottery is fired.

Kiln furniture Refractory pieces used to separate and support kiln shelves and pottery during firing.

Kneading A method of removing air pockets and dispersing moisture uniformly through clay to prepare it for use.

Latex A rubber-based glue that can be used as a peelable resist when decorating tiles.

Leather hard Clay that is stiff and damp but no longer plastic. It is hard enough to be handled without distorting but can still be decorated with slip.

Luster Metallic salts added in a thin layer over glaze to produce a lustrous metallic finish.

Majolica The name given to tin glaze earthenware with in-glaze decoration.

Monoprinting A process of transferring color and pattern to the soft clay surface—so named because the design can only be used once.

Mold A plaster former used with soft clay.

On-glaze color *See enamels*

Plastic clay Clay that can be manipulated without losing its shape.

Porcelain Fine, high-firing white clay that becomes translucent when fired.

Potter's plaster Used for making absorbent molds. The plaster hardens by chemical reaction with water. Also called plaster of Paris.

Press molding Pressing slabs of clay into molds to form shapes.

Props Tubes of refractory clay used for supporting kiln shelves during firing.

Raku A firing technique in which tiles are placed directly into a hot kiln and removed when red-hot.

Resist A decorative medium such as wax, latex, or paper used to prevent slip or glaze from sticking to the surface.

Sgraffito Scratching through a layer of clay, slip, or glaze to reveal the color underneath.

Slabbing Making tiles from slabs of clay.

Slip Liquid clay.

Slip trailing Decorating with colored slip squeezed through a nozzle.

Soaking Allowing the kiln to remain at a specific temperature for a length of time, to smooth and settle a glaze.

Soft soap A semi-liquid soap used to form a release in mold-making.

Sponging A decorative method of applying slip or glaze or cleaning the surface of tiles before firing.

Sprig A molded clay form used as an applied decoration.

Stains Unfired colors used for decorating tiles or a ceramic pigment used to add color to glazes and bodies.

Stilt Small stands used to support tiles in a firing to prevent glazed surfaces coming into contact with the kiln shelf.

Stoneware Vitrified clay, usually fired above 2,190°F (1,200°C).

Terracotta An iron-bearing earthenware clay that matures at a low temperature and fires to an earth red color.

Thermal shock Sudden increase or decrease in temperature that puts great stress on a fired clay body, causing it to crack.

Toxic Any ceramic material, raw, gaseous, or liquid, that is injurious to health.

Underglaze A color that is usually applied to either greenware or biscuit-fired tiles and in most cases covered with a glaze.

Vitrified Refers to clays which fire to high temperatures so that the clay particles fuse together and become glass-like.

Wax resist The process of decorating by painting wax on a surface to resist a water-based covering.

Wedging A method of preparing clay for use, or mixing different clays together to an even, air-free consistency.

Index

 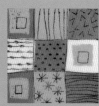

HOW TO USE THIS BOOK

Fold out this flap to find an at-a-glance guide explaining
how to navigate your way around the Tile Directory.

Credits

Author's acknowledgments

I would like to thank my daughter Charlie for her considerable contribution to the design and making of many of the tiles in this book.

I would also like to thank my daughter Nicola for her design work, my friend Charmain (Chim) Poole for her very valued contribution, Jacqui Kruzewski, and finally Ian Howes for his brilliant photography and great sense of humor.

Quarto would like to thank and acknowledge the following:

Key = a above, b below

6a   The Art Archive/Egyptian Museum, Cairo/Dagli Orti
6b   Diego Lezama Orezzoli/Corbis
7a   The Art Archive/Neil Setchfield
7b   Gérard Degeorge/Corbis
8a   Powered by Light/Alan Spencer/Alamy
8b   The Art Archive/Château de Rambouillet/Dagli Orti

All other images are the copyright of Quarto Publishing plc. While every effort has been made to credit contributors, Quarto would like to apologize should there have been any omissions or errors—and would be pleased to make the appropriate correction for future editions of the book.